CONTEMPORARY CHINA'S CULTURE

By Ouyang Xuemei

图书在版编目（CIP）数据

当代中国文化：英文 / 欧阳雪梅著；朱建廷，李莉译 . -- 北京：五洲传播出版社，2014.6

（当代中国系列 / 武力主编）

ISBN 978-7-5085-2782-6

Ⅰ.①当… Ⅱ.①欧… ②朱… ③李… Ⅲ.①文化－中国－现代－英文 Ⅳ.① G12

中国版本图书馆 CIP 数据核字 (2014) 第 124453 号

当代中国系列丛书

主　　编：武　力
出 版 人：荆孝敏
统　　筹：付　平

当代中国文化

著　　者：欧阳雪梅
译　　者：朱建廷　李　莉
责任编辑：王　峰
图片提供：中新社　CFP　FOTOE
装帧设计：丰饶文化传播有限责任公司
出版发行：五洲传播出版社
地　　址：北京市海淀区北三环中路 31 号生产力大楼 B 座 7 层
邮　　编：100088
电　　话：010-82005927，82007837
网　　址：www.cicc.org.cn
承 印 者：中煤涿州制图印刷厂北京分厂
版　　次：2014 年 6 月第 1 版第 1 次印刷
开　　本：787×1092mm 1/16
印　　张：16.25
字　　数：200 千字
定　　价：118.00 元

Contents

Preface — 6

Contemporary Chinese Culture Development and Reform — 10

    Structuring of the New China Cultural Undertakings — 12

    Achievements in Cultural Development in Early Days of New China — 23

    Rapid Development of Culture Since Reform and Opening-Up — 34

    The Path to Strengthen China Through Cultural Development in the New Century — 44

Ideology Construction — 52

    How Marxism Became the Leading Ideology — 54

    Marxism Guidance and Cultural Diversity — 65

    The Proposition of Socialist Core Values — 67

    Cultivating and Practicing Socialist Core Values — 74

Literature & Art Flourish Together — 82

Literary Creation Is in Full Swing,
Network Literature Develops Rapidly — 84

Growing Film Appeal in China — 93

New Works in Stage Art Continuously Released — 99

Cultural Construction — 106

The Construction of the Basic Framework
of a Public Cultural Service System — 108

Cultural Relic and Heritage Protection — 116

Intangible Cultural Heritage Protection — 123

Development of the Cultural Industry — 134

Initial Framework of the Cultural Market System — 136

Booming Development of the Cultural Industry — 141

The Difficulties and Potential of the Cultural
Industry Development — 146

Giving High Priority to Developing Education — 150

Building a Modern Education System — 152

Achieving Free and Compulsory Education in Both Urban
and Rural Areas — 156

Improving Fairness in Education — 158

Rapid Development of Vocational Education — 163

Popularization of Higher Education — 166

Achieving a Leap-Forward Development
of Ethnic Group Education — 171

Improvement of International Communication
and Cooperation in Education **175**

Development and Innovation of Science and Technology, Philosophy and Social Sciences — **180**

Enhancement of National Technology Innovation **182**

New Breakthrough of Science and Technology **188**

Development of Science and Technology as a Strong Support
of China's Economy and Society **193**

Prosperity and Development of Philosophy
and Social Sciences **197**

A Sound and Orderly Development of Religious Culture — **204**

Respect the Freedom of Religious Belief **206**

The Positive Role of Religions in Promoting
Social Harmony **211**

Religious Cultural Situation in Tibet **220**

International Influence of Chinese Culture — **228**

The Presentation of Chinese Culture's
"Going Global" Strategy **230**

Enriching Carriers for Cultural Exchanges **234**

Increasing China Media's Ability
to Spread to Overseas **242**

Falling Cultural Trade Deficit **247**

Conclusion — **254**

Preface

Culture is a structural concept equivalent to economics, politics and society referring to ideology, morality, literature and arts, cultural undertakings and industries, education, science and technology and religion that directly meet people's spiritual requirements. This book mainly introduces China's efforts in ideological and cultural construction, protection of people's cultural rights, forging a new morality and new social tendencies, development of literature and arts, progress in education, science and technology, philosophy and social sciences, protection of cultural heritage, the current religious situation, the structure of the cultural industry and the status of foreign cultural exchanges, and so on in the new century.

Rooted in the fertile soil of the traditional Chinese culture, contemporary Chinese culture is built on modern society. The profound 5000-year foundation of Chinese culture and the prosperity of world culture offer rich historical and cultural resources for modern cultural development. Chinese Marxism, especially the rich achievements of the socialist system with Chinese characteristics, offers valuable ideological sources for cultural construction. Since the founding of New China, especially since the reform and Opening-

Preface

up, China has promoted production, spread and consumption of culture and enhanced cultural strengths relying on sustained development of economic strength, scientific and technological competitiveness and international cultural exchanges. Society has paid growing attention and show enthusiasm in participating in cultural construction, creating a favorable social atmosphere for cultural construction. The rapid growth of spiritual and cultural needs of people has carved out a large space for cultural development. China's international position and influence has improved significantly. The diversity of world culture has attracted more attention since the late 20th Century, especially in the 21st Century.

All of these facts offer an important opportunity for Chinese culture to go global. China is facing a hard-won historical opportunity in cultural development. China has included cultural construction into the general structure of socialist undertakings with Chinese characteristics, and deployed and implemented cultural construction with economic development, political development, social development and ecological civilization development, significantly improving the status of the culture. The Chinese government has put the development of national culture in a modern view to promote the modernization of Chinese culture, develop a core value system of socialism and pool struggling forces. China has made great efforts in developing a national, scientific and popular contemporary Chinese culture towards modernization, the world and the future. The interpretation of the cultural industry enriches the content of cultural products and meets needs of the people in social cultural life. The concept of allowing all flowers to bloom together is to develop literature and arts while the concept of rejuvenating the country through science and technology is to promote the development of science and technology. Efforts have been made to protect the national cultural heritage and pass on Chinese civilization.

Contemporary China's Culture

The development of contemporary Chinese culture is an important symbol of the progress of Chinese civilization. China's achievements in contemporary Chinese culture are witnessed by the world. Efforts in promoting cultural sharing have facilitated the valuing and execution of citizens' rights in culture and education. On the basis of cultural reform, China has built the world's largest public cultural service system and the world's largest radio, TV and internet system, extending the cultural antennae to the most natural villages and the most remote bordering villages across its 9.60 million square kilometers of territory. This largest developing country with 80% illiteracy has realized popularization of higher education. China is the world's largest producer of newspapers and magazines and television plays and the third largest movie producer, with the main cultural products and cultural service size ranking among the top in the world to meet the needs of 1.3 billion people, or one fifth of the total population of the world while making contributions to people across the world.

Culture has been integrated into national economic and social development and the cultural industry has become a new growth point of the national economy and increased the brand value and material products, added value and cultural content of the modern service industry. In 1999, the term "cultural industry" entered the view of Chinese people. In 2013, legal entities in the cultural industries realized RMB2.1 trillion of added value, or 3.77% of GDP, contributing 5.5% to the economic aggregate that year.

China's cultural reform and development significantly improved the ideological and moral qualities, scientific and technological qualities of the nation, enhanced comprehensive development of people, the soft strengths of culture of China and played an irreplaceable role in the economic and social development of China. It has gradually geared into the international innovation network, and is acquiring, creating and sharing knowledge at the forefront of science and technology. In terms of the outer space exploration, China is willing to share the opportunities of carrying out scientific experiments in space and technological experiments in a future space station stage with other countries and regions.

All of the facts mentioned above show that China has become a genuine cultural power.

Contemporary Chinese Culture Development and Reform

After the founding of New China, the Chinese people have been seeking comprehensive progress in the material economy and spiritual culture. In September 1949, Mao Zedong, the newly elected chairman of the People's Republic of China, pointed out at the first plenary session of the Chinese People's Political Consultative Conference (CPPCC): "With the coming of the economic development boom, it is inevitable to see an upsurge of cultural development. The times that the Chinese people were regarded as uncivilized have gone and we will stage the world as a nation with a high degree of culture."

Zhou Enlai, premier of the State Council, made a vivid metaphor: "Economic development and cultural development are two wheels of a cart and supplement each other."

Structuring of the New China Cultural Undertakings

In the early days after the founding of New China, many things needed to be done. Structuring the cultural and educational undertakings that adapted to the new economic and political development requirement were the first task of cultural development. The *Common Program of the Chinese People's Political Consultative Conference*, equivalent to a temporary constitution, clearly put forward the need to develop "national, scientific and popular culture and education."

Renovating the Old Cultural Undertakings, Setting Up and Developing New Cultural Institutions and Facilities

Before the founding of New China, the vast territory of China lacked decent cultural facilities, except in some large and medium coastal cities, and cultural life was extremely poor in rural area and regions inhabited by ethnic groups in particular. The newly established government tried to recover and rectify the existing cultural undertakings and set up and developed new cultural institutions and facilities that adapted to needs of the people. The central government has attached great importance to developing literature and arts in the vast rural, industrial, mining and border areas and regions inhabited by ethnic groups and gradually set up a nationwide cultural network. Since 1953 cultural undertakings have been included into the Five Year Plan of the Economic and Social Development of China.

Systematic and prudent renovation of old cultural undertakings. The typical practice was to rally artists, renovate old operas and reform the old

Contemporary Chinese Culture Development and Reform

People's Publishing House is a comprehensive press, which publishes books on philosophy and social sciences. It is established in December 1950.

management system. Chinese operas had long been active at the festivals and daily life of the common people as the most typical form of art with national characteristics and a large number of folk theatric troupes. On April 3, 1951, the Chinese Opera Institute was established in Beijing and Mei Lanfang, famous Peking Opera artisit, acted as president of the institute. Mao Zedong wrote the inscription for the institute: "Allowing flowers to bloom together and getting rid of the stale and bringing forth the fresh", encouraging coexistence and development of various forms of opera.

On May 5, Premier Zhou Enlai signed an instruction on opera reform and clearly put forward the principle of reforming operas, artists and system to mine and sort traditional programs, eliminate various toxins in the old programs, use old artistic talents freely and help them improve the political awareness and artistic quality while giving play to their specialty and advantages; reform the irrational system of old theatric troupes and set up a democratic management

Contemporary China's Culture

From July 2nd to July 19th in 1949, the First National Literature Figure and Artists Conference was held in Beijing, on which China Federation of Literary and Art Circles was established. Guo Moruo was elected as chairman, Mao Dun and Zhou Yang as vice chairmen.

system. Referring to the experiences of the former Soviet Union, China set up a batch of new art troupes such as the China National Peking Opera Company, the China National Opera House, China National Orchestra, and the Beijing People's Arts Troupe. Private theatric troupes became state-owned troupes and the livelihood of the artists was guaranteed.

In July 1949, the First Session of the All China Literary and Artistic Workers Congress was convened and the China Federation of Literary and Art Circles (CFLAC) and associations of various sectors were set up to mobilize literary and artistic workers to actively take part in the cultural and arts undertakings. In the beginning of 1953, the CFLAC, China Writers Association, and associations of fine art, music, opera, movie and dance were restructured and associations of literary and artistic circles were set up in various provinces and municipalities. New China began to introduce ballet, symphony, opera, painting and other western classical arts, set up arts education systems and fostered a large number of outstanding literary talents.

Setting Up a Modern Education System and Popularizing Basic Education

Ancient China had a good education tradition and the ancient imperial examination system was an example to western countries. Some sinologists said: "The unique system in world history fostered and created an elite class which was unique in the world." [1]

However, before 1949, the poverty-stricken people who were the majority of the population had no access to education and the illiteracy rate was very high, especially in rural areas where the illiteracy rate was above 95%. According to statistics of the Education Ministry of the Kuomintang government, students of various kinds of schools only accounted for 5.6% of the population and the gross enrollment of higher education was only 0.26%.

The *Common Program of the CPPCC* put forward to popularize education

Portray of Confucius

in a planned and proper way, strengthened secondary education and higher education, emphasized technical education and enforced the spare-time education of workers and on-the-job education of cadres. In December 1949, the Ministry of Education convened the first national education working conference, formulated the guidelines and steps of gradually reforming the old education system and decided the general policy that education must serve national construction and schools must be opened to workers and farmers. The government attached great importance to the role of education in improving lives.

New China took two measures in popularizing education. The first was to completely change the situation that the majority of workers, farmers and their children were deprived of the right and chance of an education and allow adults who had no chance to receive an education access to cultural education of various degrees. The second was to set up a standard modern education system,

In July 2007, Chinese Ministry of Education announced that after ten years' education for literacy, the number of adult illiteracy has reduced by about 100 million, which is a historical breakthrough. The picture is Shanghai Book Fair.

formally include early childhood education into the education system, change primary school education to a five-year term, improve junior and senior high school systems and set up special training courses, college, undergraduate and graduate courses in universities. Schools were designed to be linked together to foster and deliver talents for national construction. The study and living expenses for students of all higher education schools, secondary education schools, normal schools and workers' and farmers' speed-up schools were funded by the government. Secondary schools also granted stipends to and reduced or exempted tuitions of the poverty-stricken students to ensure the majority of working people and their children to have access to education. In addition, the government also selected students and interns to study in the former Soviet Union and east Europe to foster the backbone of the senior leadership and new technical experts that were needed in national construction.

Old China had a small number of higher learning institutions and the distribution was not reasonable. In the second half of 1951, the central

Tian Guiying, female driver and national model worker introduced study experience to her lower classmates in Industry and Agriculture Speed-up Education Middle School of Northeast College of Engineering in the1950s.

Contemporary China's Culture

In recent years, Jingxi County in Guangxi Province has increased input in compulsory education, and improved school condition, effectively solving the difficulties in enrollment for poverty-stricken minority students in border areas.

government began to make a planned comprehensive adjustment to higher learning institutions. The general policy was: centering on fostering talent for industrial development and teachers, efforts shall be made to develop dedicated institutes and colleges, rectify and enforce development of comprehensive universities, gradually create correspondence schools and night universities to create conditions for enrolling a large number of workers and farmers in the higher learning institutions. To meet the needs of industrialization, some universities set up atomic energy, semiconductor, electronics and automation and other new technology specialties.

The door of culture was opened to the general public, completely breaking the structure that the intellectual elite monopolized culture. By 1952, worker and farmer students accounted for more than 80% of students in primary schools, about 60% of secondary schools and more than 20% of higher education.

Contemporary Chinese Culture Development and Reform

To change the backwardness of cultural education in the areas inhabited by ethnic groups and foster ethnic cadres, the Party and the Chinese government attached special importance to education in ethnic groups. In August 1951, the Ministry of Education convened the first national education conference and decided to set up nationalities universities, ethnic administrators training courses and schools in Beijing and many other cities, in addition to enforcing primary education and adult education to the minority population in areas inhabited by ethnic groups. The universities exercised apriority admission policy for students of ethnic groups. The central government also offered special help to the education of ethnic groups. For ethnic groups with their own universal characters, the language of the ethnic groups was to be used in teaching. In April 1952, the Government Administration Council promulgated the *Decision on Setting up Minority Education Administrations*, requiring the central government and the local governments set up minority education administrations or appoint dedicated personnel to take charge of the education of ethnic groups.

Chinese Academy of Sciences (CAS) is the highest academic institution in China. It is a complex research and development center of natural science and high tech.

Contemporary China's Culture

Vigorously Developing Science and Technology

The Old China not only faced backward R&D, but also had incomplete institutions, shortages of talents and funding. In 1949, there were less than 50,000 technical personnel and less than 500 natural science researchers out of only 30 dedicated research institutions.

On November 1, 1949, New China set up the Chinese Academy of Sciences as the highest academic leadership organ and key research center of China. In 1950, the Government Administration Council promulgated the *Decisions on Awarding Productive Invention, Technical Improvement and Reasonable Suggestions* and set up the All-China Federation of Natural Science Societies (ACFNSS) and All-China Science and Technology Popularization Association (ACSTPA). China set up a batch of libraries, publishing houses, various academic newspapers and designed a professional title evaluation system, established graduate fostering system and natural science prizes. With several years of development, China had more than 400,000 scientific and technical personnel, more than 800 dedicated scientific research institutes by the end of 1955. China set up a relatively complete scientific and technological organization system and technical infrastructure.

Protecting Cultural Heritage

Among the four ancient civilizations of the world (Egypt, Babylon, Chinese and Indian civilizations), only the Chinese Civilization has never been interrupted by foreign cultures. By the end of November 1948 before the founding of New China, the Pingjin Battle started. In order to protect the ancient capital of Beiping, the Party took the principle of "combining military action with negotiation and promoting negotiation by military actions" to try to protect Beiping from the flame of war and invited ancient architecture expert Liang Sicheng to mark the location of important cultural heritage and ancient buildings on the map to keep such buildings from gunfire. With efforts

Contemporary Chinese Culture Development and Reform

JiaYeTang Library in Nanxun, the ancient town in Huzhou, Zhejiang Province is the largest private library both in scale and quantity of books in modern China.

of various parties, Beiping was liberated peacefully and the cultural heritage was preserved. In 1949, the People's Liberation Army marched southwards. On May 7, Zhou Enlai sent a letter to the Department of Publicity of the Central Committee of the CPC, requiring the army to give "special protection" to the Lius' Jiayetang Library of Nanxun Town, Zhejiang Province, and Pushan Temple which housed the Tripitaka of sculpture moraine sand version of the Southern Song Dynasty in Taiyuan. The former was a private library housing more than 600,000 books. The Department of Publicity compiled and printed the *Short List of Ancient Buildings of China* and distributed the booklet to the army for special protection to these buildings. Many cultural monuments were preserved for this reason.

After the founding of New China, the Government Administration Council promulgated laws and orders and set up institutions to prohibit smuggling of cultural heritage abroad and damage domestically, changing a long history of Chinese cultural heritage being robbed and damaged. The Ministry of Culture established the State Administration of Cultural Heritage and institutes of archaeology, museums, monuments, ancient building protection institutes in various cities to take charge of cultural heritage surveys, excavation, research and protection, and housing, maintenance, research and exhibition of heritage collections. In 1960, the State Council adopted the *Interim Measures for the Cultural Heritage Protection and Management* and the list of the first batch of 180 state priority protected sites.

Achievements in Cultural Development in Early Days of New China

The full implementation of the cultural policies of New China has brought along a new situation for cultural development.

Great Achievements in Cultural Undertakings Development and Literary and Artistic Creation

With the development of three Five-Year Plans, China published 20,143 books with 2.171 billion copies, up two times from the total in 1950 and the book supply grew 7.8 times. The number of professional artistic performance organizations grew to 3465, an increase of 2465 compared with that of 1949, involving ethnic traditional dramas, modern opera, opera, singing and dancing of various ethnic groups, folk opera, acrobatics, shadow puppet, puppet shows, ballet, symphony etc. The number of theaters reached 2524, an increase of 1633 against 1949. And China had set up 22 art colleges and the number of secondary art schools increased to 59 with 11,000 students in school.

Nonprofit cultural institutions experienced great development. The number of public libraries increased to 577, an increase of 522 compared with that in 1949. The quantity of museums increased by 193 compared with 1949. The country set up 62 public art centers which were responsible for collecting, sorting and introducing folk arts, researching and guiding public art activities, 2598 cultural centers and 2125 cultural stations that were responsible for publicizing culture and arts, scientific knowledge and offering tutorship for the spare-time cultural activities for the grassroots units. The whole country has 78 radio stations, 2181 county radio stations with 96% of counties covered by

Contemporary China's Culture

Statistics show that by August 2005, the average number for Chinese people to have a public library is 459,000. The number of books in public library is 400 million, 0.3 per capita, much lower than the standard of 2 per capita made by International Federation of Library Associations (IFLA).

the cable radio services. In May 1958, the first radio station of China started to operate. Later 13 radio stations were set up. The film projection units reached 20,363, extending movie services from the urban to rural area.

The new era stimulated the enthusiasm for creation among literary and artistic workers. They created a batch of works that reflected the new era, new figures and new life and were well received. In the first film of New China *Bridge*, workers appeared on screen as masters for the first time. The representative works of that time included the modern drama *Longxugou*, the oil paintings *Founding Ceremony* and *Beautiful Mountains and Rivers*, the music-dance epic *The East is Red*, the modern drama the *White-Haired Girl*, the *Story of Miss Jiang* and *Honghu Red Guards*, the ballet *Red Detachment of Women* and the violin concerto *Liang Shanbo and Zhu Yingtai*, and many others.

In this period, achievements were made in sorting and reform of the

Contemporary Chinese Culture Development and Reform

Show of *The East Is Red*, a grand musical, 1964.

traditional drama heritage. From June 1956 to April 1957, the country found and recorded nearly 10,000 programs and sorted 4223 programs and staged 1052 plays. Many endangered dramas gained a new life, best represented by Kunju Opera. A batch of outstanding plays such as the *Harmony between General and Minister*, *Legend of White Snake*, *Fifteen Strings of Coppers*, *Woman Generals of the Yangs*, and the *Goddess Marriage* were created and are staged to this today.

Guo Moruo, Maodun, Fan Wenlan, Jian Bozan, Ba Jin, Lao She, Cao Yu, Zhao Shuli, Xu Beihong, Qi Baishi, Mei Lanfang and some other social scientists, writers and artists became renowned at home and abroad.

A Poor Country to Run a Big Educational System

New China made great efforts in popularizing basic education. In the first Five-Year Plan period, China spent RMB 7.664 billion in education and RMB 1.622 billion yuan in education infrastructure, accounting for 2.3% of the gross national income and 6.9% of fiscal spending. By 1965, China had developed 1.6819 million primary schools with 116.209 million students; and the enrollment rate of school-age children was 84.7%. There were also 181,020 secondary schools with 9.3379 million students, 7294 vocational schools with 1.2665 million students and 434 higher learning institutions with 674,000 students. The illiteracy rate declined from 80% in the early days of liberation to about 43%. By the end of 1970s, the illiteracy rate dropped to 16.4% in the urban area and 34.7% in the rural area. The significant improvement of the education level offered important support for socialist construction and gained a good reputation in the international community. Former Prime Minister of France Pierre Mendès France said: "In New China, the issue of schools is given priority." Nobel laureate Amartya Sen (1998) concluded that education in the early days of New China laid a foundation for the economic takeoff of China after the reform and Opening-up, saying education in 20-plus years offered talents for the rapid industrialization while completing education popularization to the general public.

Jiunaishan Primary School of Liuku town in Lushui County, Nujiang prefecture, Yunnan Province.

Contemporary Chinese Culture Development and Reform

Impressive Achievements in Development of Science and Technology

New China quickly fostered "a sizable team of excellent scientific and technological experts". By means of retaining and educating intellectuals of Old China, luring and settling returned experts and fostering the new generation of technological personnel, China made up the shortage of technological talents and managed to build scientific and technological talent. By the end of 1956, a total of 1805 scientists returned from abroad, including Qian Xuesen, Zhao Zhongyao, Yang Chengzhong, Cheng Kaijia, Huang Kun, Deng Jiaxian, Fu Ying, Tang Aoqing, Cao Tianqin, Hua Luogeng, Wu Tianjun, Hou Xianglin, Li Siguang and Ye Duzheng and other leading scientists. Most of them became pacemakers of the cutting-edge areas and the weak and blank fields. By 1965, China had 2.458 million technical workers, including 16,000 holders of master

Zhou Enlai, former premier of China, was having a cordial talk with the famous geologist Li Siguang in 1952. Under the care of the premier, Li Siguang came back to China and worked as vice president of CAS at the end of 1949.

certificates and 1.13 million with university education. There were 1714 professional research institutions with 120,000 scientific and technological researchers in various fields and sectors.

At the beginning of 1956, the Central Committee of the CPC convened a national intellectual conference and issued a call to march towards science and technology. Later the Chinese government organized more than 600 scientists to discuss and formulate the *1956–1967 Long-term Plan for the Scientific and Technological Development*. The plan was completed in 1962 ahead of schedule. The following year, the *1963–1972 Plan for Scientific and Technological Development* was implemented. These plans focused on science and technology related to food, clothing and utility and cutting-edge science and technology for national defense. At the same time, the technical problems in the basic industry were addressed.

On October 16th, 1964, the first atomic bomb developed by China has its first explosion successfully.

On June 17th, 1967, the first hydrogen bomb developed by China has its first explosion successfully.

China Adopted the Policy of Combining Advanced Science and Technology from Abroad with Independent Research and Development

In February 1950, China and the former Soviet Union signed agreements, causing the former Soviet Union to send experts and technicians to China and introducing technology and equipment by means of reciprocity transactions. In the First Five-Year Plan period (1953–1957), China received support from the former Soviet Union in the scientific and technological development. However, since the 1960s, China relied on independent innovation in core and key technologies. From the 1960s to the 1970s, China boosted development of the information engineering, system engineering, telemetering, remote sensing, remote control precision machining, automation, simulation and the other high and new technologies with research and development of the cutting-edge weapons such as atomic bomb and missiles. Such efforts also drove development of mathematics, physics, chemistry and other basic science and mechanics, electronics, optics, acoustics, aerodynamics, hydrodynamics and other applied sciences, improved the modern technological system and the level of science and technology. Progress in science and technology vigorously promoted development in the economy and secured the people's health.

New social tendencies

The Party made serving the people its tenet and advocated a morality of loving the motherland, people, labor, science and public property. It carried out a great reform of transforming social traditions and eradicating the old and fostering the new, further consolidating interpersonal relationships of mutual equality and mutual respect. The moral tendency of being honest, hard working and struggling prevailed with model workers appearing in all sectors. Lei Feng was a representative. He did well at an ordinary post and became an idol of the youth as a thrifty, helpful, volunteering and industrious young man. In March

Contemporary China's Culture

On March 20th, 2014, people from all around China visited Jiao Yulu Memorial in Lankao, Henan Province.

1963, the *People's Daily* and the *PLA Daily* published the inscriptions of Mao Zedong and the other state leaders on learning from Lei Feng. Programs learning from Lei Feng were carried out across the country, vigorously promoting the formation of the healthy and active social tendency.

In Old China men and women were unequal. In contrast, New China had female tractor drivers and train drivers. "Women hold up the half sky" was a popular slogan of that time and a portrait of liberated women.

New China was active in expanding foreign cultural exchanges while building a new culture. For western cultures, Mao Zedong advocated "adapting foreign things to Chinese needs" and "China shall absorb advanced foreign cultures as the raw materials of our own culture".

During the Cold War period, China held extensive exchanges and

Contemporary Chinese Culture Development and Reform

On March 2nd, 2011, three days before Lei Feng's Day, some subway stations in Shanghai hung posts of Leifeng, making it a unique landscape.

cooperation with socialist countries, developing countries in Asia, Africa and Latin America and some western countries in the fields of literature, arts, education, sports, healthcare, science and technology, news, publication, radio, film, cultural heritage, book and museum. In 1964, China established diplomatic ties with France and signed cultural exchange plans between 1956 and 1966 with the French government. That was the first inter-governmental cultural exchange plan China made with a western European country.

In 1971 China resumed its seat in the United Nations and foreign cultural exchanges were expanded. The symbolic event was the Excavated Cultural Heritage Exhibition of the People's Republic of China that started in May 1973. The exhibition was held in 15 countries and regions, including France, Japan, the UK, the U.S., Philippines and Australia and the exhibits included treasures

Contemporary China's Culture

"Horse Stepping on Flying Swallow", the bronze galloping horse, treasure of Gansu Museum was unearthed in Han dynasty tombs at Leitai, Wuwei, Gansu Province in 1969. It has been elected as symbol of Chinese tourism industry in 1985.

such as the jade clothes sewn with gold wire, Horse Stepping on a Flying Swallow, and bronze bells that could reflect the long history and wisdom of the Chinese people.

The five-year exhibition attracted more than 6.5 million visitors across the world, shocking the world, and was regarded as "cultural heritage diplomacy". The exhibit stayed in the UK more than 4 months, attracting 770,000 visitors. Then British Prime Minister Edward Heath attended the opening ceremony and delivered a speech. Queen Elizabeth II visited the exhibition.

New China also faced setbacks in cultural development. In the "Anti-Rightist Movement" in 1957 and a batch of intellectuals were wrongly classified as "rightists". The "Cultural Revolution" started in 1966. Most

Copper chime exhibited in "National Treasure" fair held in Hainan Museum on April 1st, 2009.

literary and artistic organizations were forced to dismiss and cultural facilities were destroyed. China experienced cultural hard times with "800 million people watching eight model operas".

Contemporary China's Culture

Rapid Development of Culture Since Reform and Opening-up

After the end of the "Cultural Revolution" in 1976, China entered into times of reform and Opening-up and culture gained a new life and started to recover and develop. The debate on criteria of truth started in May 1978 and the 3rd Plenary Session of the 11th National Congress of the CPC convened in December of the same year marking the start of reform and Opening-up and a new stage in the ideological and cultural construction of China.

The significance of the debate on criteria of truth not only lied on clarifying the common sense of theories. More importantly, it emancipated peoples' minds and solved the question of how to study the actual situation of

On December 18th, 1978, the Third Plenary Session of the 11th Central Committee of the Chinese Communist Party was solemnly opened in Beijing, stating a new historical period of reform and Opening-up.

China with Marxist theories. Therefore the debate became the starting point of bringing order out of chaos in the ideological and cultural field. At the fourth national congress of literary and art circles convened at the end of October 1979, Deng Xiaoping delivered a speech. He fully confirmed the achievements made in the literary and artistic sector since the founding of New China, put forward to promote free development of artistic creation both in forms and styles and the thinking of allowing free discussion of different viewpoints and schools regarding to the artistic theories. He put forward the missions in the new period: "We shall improve the level of science and technology and culture, develop gracious and colorful cultural life and build a high level of socialist spiritual civilization while developing a high level of material civilization."

The literary and artistic creation in forms such as modern drama, reportage, poetry, films, short stories, comedy, cross-talk, comics and architecture fresco emerged like bamboo shoots after a spring rain, reflecting

On November 21st, 2002, "Give Heart to the Readers" celebration was co-organized by Shanghai Writers' Association and Harvest Literature Magazine, celebrating the fortieth anniversary of *Harvest*'s first issue.

the great enthusiasm of writers and artists. They created unprecedented prosperity of culture. In 1981, the amount of distribution of periodicals of literature and arts hit 1.2 billion copies. The circulation of the *Contemporary Era* and *October of Beijing*, *Harvest* of Shanghai, *Kunlun* of the PLA, *Zhongshan* of Nanjing and the *Flower City* of Guangzhou all reached hundreds of thousands of copies. From October 1976 to September 1982, China published nearly 1500 novelettes and more than 500 full-length novels, created about 4200 modern dramas and operas (including adaptations) and published more than 500 kinds of poetry collections and more than 40,000 poems each year.

Since 1981, the country saw production of more than 100 films each year. With the popularization of TV sets, TV plays developed rapidly. A batch of outstanding works emerged in the fine arts, dancing and Quyi and other fields. Promising young writers and artists in the circles of literature and arts emerged in the 1970s and 1980s became a very active fresh troops and created increasingly diversified artistic expression forms and styles. Importance was attached to absorbing the active results of foreign cultures while promoting the national outstanding cultural traditions in the cultural development of this period.

In this period, academic thinking was very active, emerging comparisons between traditional Chinese culture and western cultures, study and discussion on relations between traditional Chinese culture and China's modernization, forming a "cultural fever" that attracted attention and participation from all walks of life. The discussions and debates urged people to think, expanded their horizons and deepened study of Chinese people in cultural issues.

Meanwhile, some literary and artistic works showed bad tendencies, such as dark and grey descriptions and reckless invention, misrepresentation of history and denials of reality. Facing the new situation and new problems, the Chinese leaders sought to enforce the development of a socialist spiritual

Contemporary Chinese Culture Development and Reform

civilization. At the 12th National Congress of the CPC convened in September 1982, spiritual civilization was defined as one of the important factors of socialism. The Central Committee of the CPC reached two decisions in 1986 and 1996 on the construction of a socialist spiritual civilization, elaborated and deployed the strategic position, guideline, principles, missions and objectives of the spiritual civilization in socialist development with Chinese characteristics.

On February 25, 1981, the movement of "five stresses and four points of beauty", jointly initiated by nine units, including the All-China Federation of Trade Unions, the Central Committee of the Communist Youth League and the All-China Women's Federation, was carried out. The movement centered on stresses on decorum, manners, hygiene, discipline and morals and beauty of the mind, language, behavior and the environment, becoming the opening chapter of the construction of a public spiritual civilization in the new period. The

On October 9th, 2012, winner of the 12th "Five Ones" Project Award (a good book, a good TV series, a good play, a good film, a good article), *Eight Sons Jointing the Army* playing its show in Beijing. It is a large-scale opera adapted from real story of young men and women enthusiastically joining the army happened in south region of Jiangxi Province.

Contemporary China's Culture

On January 9th, 2014, service activity of "culture, science, and health going to the rural areas" was held in culture hall at Zhongxie village in Jidong town. The activity was started by Jikeqiao District committee in Shaoxing, Zhejiang Province. During the activity, the group provided service such as writing spring festival scrolls, free clinic, introducing science related knowledge, legal consulting and an entertainment show.

initiative was strongly supported by the government and the public responded actively. Tens of millions of CYL members, young people, servicemen and college students provided various knowledge consulting services and labor services to help those that were in difficulty.

Entering into the 1990s, China made new achievements in the construction of a spiritual civilization. The central government initiated the "Five Ones" Project,[2] appraisal encouraging the efforts to creating outstanding works that advocate the spirit of the times and could be highly received by the public. In order to allow rural areas to share the high quality cultural resources of urban areas, 10 ministries and commissions of the central government jointly organized the project of "bringing cultural, technological and healthcare services to the rural area" at the end of 1996 to promote cultural construction

Contemporary Chinese Culture Development and Reform

in rural areas. The report of the 15th National Congress of the CPC explicitly pointed out that socialist modernization requires both a prosperous economy and a flourishing culture. Only with economy, politics and culture developing in harmony and the material civilization and spiritual civilization being developed well can it be called socialism with Chinese characteristics.

Since the reform and opening-up, China's cultural development started with education, science and technology. In early August 1977, Deng Xiaoping presided over two symposia on science, technology and education. He pointed out the key to scientific and technological modernization was to give priority to education of science and technology. The central government decided to resume normal scientific research and education, especially resuming college entrance examinations. Such efforts not only changed the fate of hundreds of thousands of people but also fundamentally changed the attitude of the society to knowledge and intellectuals and laid a foundation for the cultural

Picture of examination room of the 1st college entrance examination after the resuming of college entrance examination in China.

and economic development and other efforts. From the autumn of 1977 to the summer of 1978, 11.60 million people attended the college entrance examination. Deng also emphasized the idea of "allowing all schools of thoughts to contend", requiring all schools of thought to respect each other and learn from each other. He also required the running academic publications.

In March 1978, the national science conference was held in Beijing. Deng Xiaoping called for understanding of the top position of science and technology and intellectuals. He said the Party should be good at leadership and do a good job in ensuring logistics. He called for the beginning of the recovery of an effective education systems and scientific and technological research mechanisms that were effective in the past and improving the education, scientific and technological research conditions and material amenities of intellectuals. Since then "respecting knowledge and talents" became the core of policies related to intellectuals.

Encouraged and inspired by the new policies, a batch of model intellectuals with the spirit of creation, exploration and devotion were highly praised, including Chen Jingrun, Li Siguang, Hua Luogeng, Gao Shiqi, Yang Le, Zhang Guanghou, Lin Qiaozhi, Jiang Zhuying and others and their stories were widely known.

In November 1986, the Central Committee of the CPC and the State Council approved the proposal of Wang Ganchang, Chen Fangyun, Yang Jiachi and Wang Daheng, academicians of the Chinese Academy of Sciences, to implement the *Outline for the High-tech Research and Development Program*, or the "863" Project. Two years later, the high-tech industry development plan or the "Torch Program" was implemented, aiming at promoting the commercialization, industrialization and internationalization of high-tech achievements and promoting the technical renovation and industrial structure adjustment of the traditional industries. With the rollout of various plans, achievements were made in scientific and technological development and China

Contemporary Chinese Culture Development and Reform

White marble statue of Lin Qiaozhi in Yu Garden (Lin Qiaozhi Memorial) in Gulangyu, Xiamen, Fujian Province.

has acquired world-leading results in space technology, high-energy physics, biology, medicine and health, geoscience, chemistry and other important technological fields.

Education is the foundation for the development of a nation. Deng Xiaoping put forward the education objectives of "facing modernization, the world and the future". In light of the actual situation that China has a large population and the populace's cultivation was relative low, China emphasized the importance of basic education. The first step was to popularize nine-year compulsory education, recover and develop worker and farmer education and part-time education.

On April 12, 1985, the Compulsory Education Law of China was promulgated. In May 1995, the CPC Central Committee and the State Council made the *Decision on Accelerating the Scientific and Technological Progresses* and put forward the strategy of rejuvenating China through science and technology and education. In the period from 1997 to 2002, investment in education grew by 16.7% on average annually and in 2002 alone the total input reached RMB 548 billion. With strong policy support, education undertakings developed with unprecedented speed and quality.

By the end of the 20th century, the objective of popularization of the nine-year compulsory education and basically eliminating youth illiteracy had been realized. A vocational and adult education system with complete structure and disciplines has roughly taken shape. In order to improve the education level of young people, China accelerated the development of higher education and promulgated the *Higher Education Law* on August 29, 1998, enforced structural adjustments and promoted the "211" Program[3] and the "985" Program[4], aiming to build a batch of high-quality universities and promoting "teaching-oriented universities" to transfer to "research-oriented universities" and enlarged the admission size of universities in 1999.

The Second Education Forum of the 21st Century and Non-government Funded Education Summit was held in Suzhou, with the theme of "Diversity, Legalization, and Non-government Funded Education".

The rapid development of private education helped the formation of a "diversified, multi-mode, multi-tier and multi-channel" higher education system under the context of publicized education. From 1989 to 2001, the common and adult higher learning institutions of China fostered nearly 12 million students with diploma and bachelor degrees, more than 300,000 postgraduates, 3.43 million holders of diploma and bachelor certificates through self-taught examinations, delivering a large number of talents for China's modernization.

At the end of the 1970s, Deng Xiaoping pointed out that science and technology and all advanced production management experience and outstanding practices and styles were the common wealth of mankind. Every nation or country needs to learn from the other countries and from the advantages of other nations. With his proposal, China sent 480 students to 28 countries to learn in 1978. Since then, the international cooperation and exchanges have been continuously increased.

Contemporary China's Culture

The Path to Strengthen China Through Cultural Development in the New Century

From the beginning of reform and opening-up to the end of the 20th Century, China attached importance to the role of culture in its strategic structure and emphasized the socialist spiritual civilization, socialist culture with Chinese characteristics and the importance of culture as an integral part of the comprehensive strength of the country. However, in that period, economic development was still given top priority and cultural development was given a secondary position. The saying "culture building a platform for the economy to play a leading role" reflected the situation of cultural development at that time.

Entering into the new century, people realized that the soft power of

In 2012, Feng Jicai, Wang Jianlin and others discussed "deepen cultural revolution and promote the prosperity of culture" on CPPCC.

Contemporary Chinese Culture Development and Reform

culture is an important part of a country's competitiveness. At the same time, the improvement of people's living standards led to increasing demands on culture. When China entered into the critical period of building a moderately prosperous society in an all-round way, the role of culture was unprecedented.

The understanding of the importance of cultural construction advanced with the times. In 2002, the 16th National Congress of the CPC put forward the goal to vigorously develop advanced culture. In 2007, the report of the 17th National Congress of the CPC put forward the task and objective of "promoting the development and prosperity of the socialist culture" and "improving the soft power of culture". In 2011, the 6th Session of the 17th National Congress of the CPC elaborated on the socialist cultural development path with Chinese characteristics for the first time and put forward the objective of building the socialist power of culture. In 2012, the 18th National Congress of the CPC clearly put forward the strategic plan of a "five-in-one structure of economic development, political development, cultural development, social development and ecological civilization development", emphasized that the socialist

On October 24th, 2012, the second plenary meeting of 29th Session of the Eleventh Meeting of the Standing Committee of the Eleventh NPC was held in the Great Hall of the People, on which Cai Wujian, the Culture Minister made report on deepening reform of the cultural system and prodding socialistic culture to be in great development and prosperity.

advanced culture is an integral part of the "five-in-one" structure, concluded that building a moderately prosperous society in an all-round way is to benefit the 1.3 billion people of China, allow them to live an affluent material life and enjoy a healthy and rich cultural life.

The impetus of cultural development lies in reform and innovation. Accompanying the cultural concept of development is the promotion of cultural system reform. Since the reform and opening-up, cultural system reform has been gradually rolled out with a deepening economic reform and changed the existing concepts and practices of the nationalization of culture and cultural resources. In the 1990s, the CPC Central Committee clarified the goal of exploring a cultural system that adapts to the socialist market economy and the development the law of culture itself. The cultural system reform started with a funding appropriation system, promoting internal reform of artistic troupes on the one hand; and accelerated the market integration and structural adjustment with the establishment of large scale cultural groups as the breakthrough on the other hand. As a result, a batch of newspaper, publication, circulation, radio and TV and film groups were set up. The State Council also designed economic policies in 1996 and 2000 to support cultural development.

Entering into the new century, China further broke the concepts and mechanisms that constrained cultural development. In October 2000, the 5th Plenary Session of the 15th National Congress of the CPC adopted the 10th Five-Year Plan (2001–2005) and put forward the concept of a "cultural industry" for the first time, realizing a theoretic breakthrough. Culture no longer had a single attribute of ideology but dual the attributes of both ideology and commodity. Acknowledging the "dual attributes" of culture, emphasizing that the cultural industry is an important channel to flourish the socialist culture in market economic conditions and to meet the cultural needs of the public helped solve question that has long plagued people on the relationship between cultural development and the market, broke the mode that the government was responsible for everything related to cultural undertakings under the traditional planned economic system, changed the administrative distribution mode of cultural resources and the concept that cultural units were an administrative appendage. In 2001, the developing of the cultural industry was included in the 10th Five-Year Plan. The industrial functions and economic attributes of culture were widely acknowledged and culture was no longer a stepping stone towards economic development, but played a leading role in development with its relatively independent position and value.

Every theoretic breakthrough will lead to a step forward in the reform. A national cultural system reform pilot working conference convened in June 2003 and selected nine regions and 35 cultural units to carry out cultural system reform pilot programs. The Third Plenary Session of the 16th National Congress of the CPC convened in October of the same year and further clarified that different development strategies would be adopted for nonprofit cultural undertakings and the cultural industry. On the one hand, efforts would be made to vigorously develop non-profit cultural undertakings to protect people's basic cultural rights and interests. On the other hand, we would do a good job in the reform and development of the cultural industry with a focus on a market-faced system of innovation, transformation and strength improvement.

The decision to separate non-profit cultural undertakings from the cultural industry clearly defined the line between the government and the market. Nonprofit cultural undertakings will be developed with the government as the leading force, aiming to protect the basic cultural rights and interests of the masses.The cultural industry was also oriented on the market, aiming at meeting the diversified, multi-level spiritual and cultural needs of the masses. Correspondingly, the state-owned cultural units were "divided into two": one part nonprofit and the other for profit.

The cultural system reform that has lasted for more than 10 years centered on forging market players, improving the market system and macro-

On October 29th, 2010, unveiling ceremony of reform and restructure of municipal cultural institutions was held in government hall in Shangluo, Shaanxi Province.

management and transforming government functions. The reformed culture is not longer a closed cycle, but has been integrated into the "large circulation" of national economic and social development. On the one hand, the development of a cultural industry cannot be separated from the support of the national economic system; on the other hand, the cultural industry has become a new growth point as a strategic emerging industry and is integrating with the national economy, education, urban-rural construction, science and technology and tourism. Culture has penetrated all sectors and has played an irreplaceable role improving brand value, increasing material production and added value and the cultural content of the modern service industry and accelerating the transformation of economic development mode. The transformation of the governmental function is mainly reflected in the great efforts to separate the government functions from enterprise management, separating administrative units from institutional units and separating government supervision and regulation from enterprise management, allowing the government transformation from running cultural undertakings to regulating cultural development with policy adjustments, market supervision, social management and public services and from micro management to macro management. Institutional reform of the State Council in 2013 and the combination of the General Administration of Press and Publications with the State Administration of Radio, Film and Television indicated the end of cultural administration transformation. China also enforced cultural legislation construction and promulgated more than 400 laws and regulations and policies.

With the innovation of cultural concepts, the 10 plus years in the new century witnessed the fastest cultural development with deepening cultural system reform, continuous promotion of cultural legislation, systemization and improved economic strength of China.

Statistics from the Office of National Statistics showed that in 2012, value added in cultural industry reached 1807.1 billion RMB yuan, with a rise of 16.5% than that of 2011, 6.8 percentage points higher than GDP growth with the same caliber and current price. The contribution made by cultural industry to the overall growth of the economy is 5.5%.

Contemporary China's Culture

The Chinese government promulgated the *Outline for the Cultural Development Plan during the 11th Five Year Plan Period* in 2006 and the *Outline for the Cultural Reform and Development Plan during the 12th Five-Year Plan Period* in 2012 and sharply increased inputs into cultural development. The total public fiscal expenditure in cultural, sports and media development hit RMB 68.5 billion in 2006 and grew at an annual rate of 23% on average during the 11th Five-Year Plan period (2006–2010). In 2012, the figure reached RMB 225.145 billion, more than three times than in 2006. For more than 10 years, both the government and the market have driven cultural undertakings and the cultural industry to grow together and significantly boosted cultural productivity. China has made remarkable achievements in cultural construction, popularized cultural infrastructure, narrowing the gap between rural and urban cultural services and enriched cultural products. Chinese culture has gone to the world stage and China carved out a socialist cultural development path with Chinese characteristics.

Contemporary Chinese Culture Development and Reform

Explanation

1. *The Chinese Civilization has Shocked Me* (I), *Guangming Daily*, September 1, 2013

2. The appraisal has been held once a year since 1992, aiming at selecting the outstanding works produced, recommended and nominated by various provinces, autonomous regions, municipalities, ministries and commissions, the General Political Department of the PLA in the provice year on the five aspects: a good drama, a good TV play (film), a good book (in the social science field), a good theoretic article (social science) and a good song.

3. To meet the challenge of new technological revolution of the world, the Chinese government decided to pool all forces of the Central Government and the local governments to try to build a batch of universities with discipline and specialties reaching out to the leading universities in the world in the 21st century. This program was named "211" Program.

4. On May 4, 1998, Jiang Zemin, Chairman of the CPC, said:"In order to realize modernization, China shall build a number of world-leading universities". Then the Ministry of Education decided to implement the 21st Century Action Plan for Education Promotion, giving special support to some universities to create the world leading universities and high-level universities. Such efforts were named the "985" Program.

Ideology Construction

Amongst the contemporary Chinese ideologies and cultures, the most dominating ideology is Marxism. One of the priorities of contemporary Chinese ideology construction is to consolidate the leading role of Marxism and to cultivate and practice the socialist core values.

Contemporary China's Culture

How Marxism Became the Leading Ideology

There is an important historical reason why Marxism entered into China. With more than 5000 years of civilization history, Chinese people are proud of the fact that China made an indelible contribution to the progress of human civilization. However, modern times saw the rapid economic growth of the western capitalist countries, while China still remained an agricultural society and developed slowly. Thus, China lagged far behind the western capitalist countries at the dawn of modern times. In 1840, the first of the western powers invaded China utilizing their their stronger weapons and the hidden power of opium addiction. After that, China was forced to cede territory, pay indemnities

Oil painting of the Dvortsovaya Square during October Revolution in Russia, collected in Russia Politics and History Museum.

Ideology Construction

and was reduced to being a semi-colony and a semi-feudal society. The suffering Chinese people began to struggle and try to save the nation in peril. Since the dawn of the modern era, nearly all political theories and doctrines from around the world have been adopted to and experimented with in China. Unfortunately, none of them helped solve the many problems that faced China, and none of these many ideologies really took root in the country. The Russian October Revolution of 1917 verified the fact that intertwined ideologies of Marxism and Marxism-Leninism changed the history of world politics. The Chinese people who had been trying to grasp a working political ideology were attracted by this kind of ideology. Based on Marxism, many Chinese found the reasons why this nation had suffered such humiliation and simultaneously found the means to achieve liberation and rejuvenation, and thus restore the nation's dignity. These people were and still are known as Marxists.

Since Marxism was created by two Germans, Karl Marx and Frederik Engels, and thus a product of the western countries, it is impossible that for this ideology to provide a ready-made solution to China's problems. The first generation of China's Marxists, represented by Mao Zedong, determined that it was necessary to combine the universal truth of Marxism with the concrete practices of China and started the process of modifying Marxism to fit China. This has proven to be extremely tough and continues to this day (over 90 years later). The sino-ization of Marxism has created two sinicized theories—Mao Zedong Thought and the socialist theoretical system with Chinese characteristics.

Marxism offers is a kind of worldview and methodology on how to understand and change the world. Chinese Communist Party (will use CPC in below paragraphs) succeeded in leading the Chinese people to the termination of their suffering and humiliation, as well as changing the nation's destiny and realizing national independence and prosperity. These are the reasons why sinicized Marxism stands out amongst multiple ideologies and doctrines. These

Oil painting of founding of the PRC.

are also the reasons why most Chinese intellectuals not only accepted the CPC's leadership, but also acknowledged Marxism as the nation's ideological basis.

The fact that Marxism can become so universal and popular in China is related to the cultural characteristics of sinicized Marxism.

Sinicized Marxism is deeply rooted in the Chinese nation and is closely related to the nation's foundation. Chinese culture is profound and extensive, but China was invaded by foreign powers and lagged behind since modern times, so the people lost their confidence in Chinese culture. The first-generation leader of the CPC, Mao Zedong insisted on Chinese cultural inheritance. He put forward that inheriting the excellent cultural heritage of Chinese civilization was the "prerequisite of developing the new national culture and enhancing the national self-confidence". However, this does not mean that we should recommend historical revivalism. Instead, the right way to put this idea into practice is by "selecting the refined and discarding the crude".

Mao Zedong Thought includes many important contents, all of which are

Ideology Construction

On July 25th, 2005, "Source of Revolution, Exhibition of Marxist cultural and Art works" at Shanghai Police Museum.

derived from typical Chinese-style life wisdom and political wisdom dating from the traditional culture. A good example of this is "to follow a realistic and pragmatic approach", which originated from *Book of Han*. Mao Zedong combined this concept with Marxism and made it the ideological line of the CPC. Loyalty, fidelity, benevolence, and justice are traditional Chinese ethics. Mao Zedong redefined them as: loyalty and fidelity refer to being extremely loyal and filial to the majority of people, instead of the minority; benevolence refers to being beneficial to the majority; justice means that we can properly handle the matters to the majority's interests. To be specific, if we can appropriately handle the farmers' land problem and workers' eating problem, this can be called true benevolence and justice. (*On National Spiritual Mobilization Movement Motivation*). Chairman Mao briefly illustrated Marxist materialism perspective from people's perspective: the people are who created the history and the masses are real heroes, so we should make the interests of the people both our starting point and destination. Based on this, he established that to "serve the people" was the aim of the CPC. By combining the traditional cultural know-how with the new practices of the people, Mao Zedong helped illustrate and develop Marxism as well as Chinese culture. Since then, many people began to discover, understand and accept Marxism by listening to Mao's speeches and reading his works.

Mao Zedong was not very well educated, but he was both learned and knowledgeable. His political essays explain boring political concepts in a lively manner using layman's language. Besides, he had quite extensive accomplishments in philosophy, calligraphy, poetry and other aspects. The poetry containing his thought, practice, personality and individuality has attracted and edified several generations of Chinese people, and has even been spread to the greater world. In 1937, the U.S. correspondent Edgar Snow

On December 26th, 2013, collection exhibition themed "recalling the eventful years-commemorating Mao Zedong's 120th birthday" was held in Fuzhou. The "Serve the people" plaque written by Mao was exhibited.

Ideology Construction

compiled the English translation version of Mao's *Oblique, Long March* and wrote the book entitled *Red Star over China*, thus exposing Mao Zedong Thought to the whole world. After the founding of New China, a foreign poet praised Mao as "a poet who wins a new China." Since 1940s, Mao Zedong' poems have been translated into English, and then into French, Russian, German and dozens of other languages. One of German writers, Strauss once said, "Mao Zedong brought a disaster-ridden China, which had been in turbulence for decades and suffered from the most severe war to a new era. What's more, his wonderful poetry recorded the historical process of this era, so he is a really distinguished poet." This statement reveals Mao's dual identity: both a statesman and an intellectual. In the early 1970s, U.S. President Richard Nixon crossed the Pacific and visited China for the first time. When he met Mao Zedong, Nixon's first statement was: "after reading your poems and speeches, I know you are a profound philosopher."

Mao Zedong Thought effectively guided the Chinese revolution as the correct theory in both principle and experience. The Chinese Revolution ended with victory in 1949, with the establishment of new China, and the declaration to the world that— "the Chinese people have already stood up". After quickly healing the trauma of war and restoring the national economy, the CPC and Mao Zedong Thought was faced with a new challenge: how to build socialism in such a fragmented country with long history and large population, thus realizing China's national rejuvenation.

However, Mao Zedong didn't attach great importance to the relative independence of culture and ideology. Especially in the later years, he made severe mistakes in judging the cultural field and extending the class struggle. Other leads of CPC, represented by Deng Xiaoping corrected Mao's mistakes and defended his basic principle, standing point and ideas. *Resolutions for Certain Historical Issues of the Party since the Establishment of the P.R.C*, presided by Deng Xiaoping, scientifically evaluated the historical status of Mao Zedong, differentiating Mao Zedong Thought from the mistakes he made in the later

Contemporary China's Culture

From September 1st to 11th, 1982, the Twelfth National Congress of the Communist Party of China was held in Beijing, on which Deng Xiaoping put forward the idea of socialism with Chinese characteristics in the opening ceremony.

years. This Resolution made it clear that, "Mao Zedong Thought is the valuable spiritual wealth of our party, which will guide our actions for a long time".

After the Third Plenary Session of the 11th Committee of the Communist Party of China, CPC continues to promote the Marxism sinicization by adhering to Mao Zedong Thought based on China's national conditions, while trying to meet the requirements of the time, development and innovation of Marxism and Mao Zedong Thought. In 1982, during the 12th CPC National Congress, Deng Xiaoping proposed, "combine the universal truth of Marxism with the concrete realities of our country, choose our own way and build socialism with Chinese characteristics." Since then, Deng expounded the nature, fundamental task, development path, development stage, and the development momentum of socialism. Deng also discussed the external environment, political assurance, strategic steps, leadership strength, and supporting strength of socialist construction as well as questions like national reunification. He also answered

Ideology Construction

On September 20th, 2009 large-scale dancing drama "Road to Revival" made its first debut in the Great Hall of the People in Beijing. Following the historical time venation, the drama was composed of the prelude and other five chapters, which has more than 3200 actors in 36 programs.

the questions of what is socialism, how to construct socialism, how to create a socialism with Chinese characteristics, how to adopt new ideas and promote Marxism, thus bringing the new understanding of socialism to a higher scientific level.

The theoretical system of socialism with Chinese characteristics was formed after the Third Plenary Session of the 11th Committee of the Communist Party of China. It is the theoretical principle and the summary of experiences about how to construct, consolidate and develop Chinese socialism. This theoretical system includes Deng Xiaoping Theory, the important thought of "Three Represents", and Scientific Outlook on Development. The reason why the theoretical system of socialism with Chinese characteristics became the dominant idea of Chinese society lies in the influence of regime. Besides this influence, there are four other advantages: itself has a set of complete theoretical system; it bears similarity and compatibility with the universal social ideal in traditional Chinese culture; proposition in this system conforms to people's feelings and desires to revitalize the nation and promote the development of Chinese society, representing the majority Chinese people's fundamental interests; instead of copying Marxism as it is. CPC kept pace with the times and were devoted to the sinicization, modernization, and massification of Marxism. By innovating theory according to the practice development, they found their own way to construct and reform socialism, successfully realizing steady growth of comprehensive national strength as well as constant improvement of people's living standards.

In the October of 2012, the newly elected CPC collective leadership is faced with the new task of building a well-off society. Given the new situation that reform is into deeper water; development mode needs urgent change; social contradictions are highlighted; the international situation and the external environment are increasingly complex and changeable, the new leadership is expected to respond to how to insist and further enrich the Marxism with Chinese features. At the beginning of Xi Jinping's (the General Secretary of the Presidency) inauguration, he said to Chinese people, "people are yearning for a better life, which is also our goal," On Nov. 29, at the National Museum, which is the equivalent of "Confucian temples", where people cherish the memory of the history of the nation, Xi Jinping announced "Chinese dream" to the world— "to achieve the great rejuvenation of the Chinese nation has been the greatest dream since the modern times."

The Connotation of Chinese dream is to achieve national prosperity, revitalization, and the people's happiness. The Chinese dream should primarily refer to the dream of China's rejuvenation. After 100 years of endeavor, China's chronic poverty situation has been improved greatly. But this objective (China's rejuvenation) has not been achieved yet. Chinese dream should secondly refer to the dream of Chinese nation's rise. China is supposed to regain its self-

Ideology Construction

reliance and independence among the nations, become integrated with the world, become equal members amongst all the world nationalities, enjoy the due status and dignity, and make corresponding contribution with China's 1.3 billion people and 5000 years of the civilization history. In addition, the Chinese dream includes the dream of a Chinese cultural Renaissance.

Chinese culture played the leading cultural role around the world for the greater part of world history. For now, how to successfully convert to a modern form from the classical form, how to realize the Chinese cultural in heritage and innovation, and how to present a brand-new style and features of the times have become big issues for the Chinese people to resolve. The Chinese dream is a personal development dream for every individual, providing more equal conditions and opportunities for personal fulfillment, of which the ultimate goal is to finally realize the free and comprehensive development for human beings and benefit every individual, the country and the whole nation. The Chinese dream is the dream of the contemporary Chinese social development and progress, which vividly summarizes the people's pursuit since modern times and directly expresses China's development goals in the 21st century.

The Chinese dream caused heated debate around the world. There was an article in the American magazine *News Week* stating that the Chinese dream will exert a profound influence and will definitely "revive the Chinese glorious history". A foreign observer keenly noted that this is "a goal that can arouse resonance among people", and this dream reflects the CPC's "strong sense of responsibility towards Chinese nation."

Twenty years ago, an American scholar Fukuyama claimed that the disintegration of the Berlin Wall and the collapse of Soviet socialism is a sure sign of the end of Marxism. However, in the past 20 years, CPC established "two hundred targets", from "building a well-off society" to "building a moderately prosperous China". China is striding towards national rejuvenation with a dramatical speed. Fukuyama therefore revised his point of view. He said that the objective facts prove that Western-style liberal democracy may not be the end of the evolution of human history, as China continues to rise, China may still prove to be the treasure house and soul of human thought.

Here are some comments from an Australian scholar Hugh White:

"We should admit that China is undergoing a lot of good things. Since China has achieved economic growth, hundreds of millions of Chinese people live a better and more prosperous life that their parents had never dreamed of before. These material conditions including better housing, better schools and better health care bear real ethical value. If you don't admit these achievements, the only reason is that you are being dishonest."

In the past 30 years, China has successfully brought 400 million people out of poverty and brought all 1.3 billion people toward modernization. China's annual average contribution rate to the world economy has exceeded 20%, which is "real ethical value" to the Chinese development mode. Sinicized Marxism has become a kind of wonderful scenery in the garden of world culture, adding to the splendor of the treasure house of human culture.

In the past over 90 years, Sinicized Marxism has changed the fate of hundreds of millions of Chinese people. Despite that there are many deficiencies, most Chinese people have confidence in socialist theory, and the socialist system with Chinese characteristics. CNN.com recently reported that Millward Brown statistics indicate that about 70% Chinese think it is important to realize Chinese Dream and stress that the realization of national honor instead of individual achievements is the key to that.

Marxism Guidance and Cultural Diversity

Culture is a mix of spiritual flowers, and China is a big family composed of 56 nationalities with more than one billion population. The cultural background, cultural requirements, and cultural appeals of various ethnic groups, regions, social groups and individuals are quite diverse. Thus China will embrace the cultural diversity while adhering to the guidance of Marxism.

From the source, Sinicized Marxism has absorbed the Chinese civilization, Marxism, Western capitalist civilization and other cultural nutrients. In terms of the development process, the New China has always accepted China's cultural diversity. After establishing Marxism as the guiding role, Mao Zedong pointed out in May 1956: "letting a hundred flowers blossom and a hundred schools of thought contend" is the guiding principle of China's development of science and prosperity of literature and art. In 1957, he delivered two speeches in February and March to further explain this concept. He said:

"Different forms and styles of art are supposed to develop freely and different schools are free to contend. If we use administrative power to impose some art styles and schools while forbid others, it will be detrimental to the development of art and science. That is to say, the right and wrong in art and science should be discussed freely within the community instead of being defined by some simple rules."

Mao believed that the implementation of this policy will not undermine the Marxist guidance. On the contrary, it would strengthen its guiding role. He had repeatedly stated that this is a basic, long-term approach, instead of a temporary policy. Adhering to the guidance of Marxism and the "double hundred" policy went hand in hand for a long time, and continues to this day.

Marxism is only a kind of guidance instead of monopolization or enforcement. After the beginning of reform and Opening-up, Chinese leaders made it clear that carrying forward the theme of the times and promoting diversity is a basic requirement of advanced socialist culture. Carrying forward the theme means that we should advocate all the thoughts and ideas in favor of promoting patriotism, collectivism, socialist reform, Opening-up, modernization, national unity, social progress, and people's happiness. This is an essential requirement of socialist system during cultural construction, a concrete manifestation of socialist spiritual civilization, and a kind of social responsibility that socialist culture must shoulder. Implementation of the "double hundred" policy and promoting diversity are the objective requirements of the basic conditions for the primary stage of socialism cultural construction proposed by the growing diverse, multi-level, multi-faceted spiritual and cultural needs of people, where the motivation of socialist culture development lies.

Adhering to the guidance of Marxism and cultural diversity is a completely unified thought. Ultimately, Marxism guides the soul of socialist culture. However, this does not necessarily mean that every cultural product should embody Marxism. On the contrary, Marxism encourages diverse cultural styles and contents. So does the Chinese traditional culture, which absorbs a lot of achievements of other civilizations like Buddhism, eventually forming a forming an open cultural pattern. Chinese society welcomes all the works and behaviors beneficial to prosperity and development of socialist construction, revitalization of the nation, the country's prosperity, people's happiness and social harmony; regardless of Marxism or non-Marxism, materialism or idealism, secular or religious ideas. Currently, there are 85 million CPC members who believe in Marxism and over 100 million people who believe in various religions.

The Proposition of Socialist Core Values

The term core values refers to the ideology, ethics and values that could embody the fundamental interests of the principal members in the community, and reflect the main value demands of the community members, as well as maintain or promote social reform and progress. The CPC attaches great importance to nurturing and cultivating such core values by proposing the construction of the Socialist Spiritual Civilization after the reform and opening-up policy. Deng Xiaoping pointed out: "Spiritual Civilization, not only refers to education, science, culture (which are absolutely necessary), but also refers to communist ideology, principles, ideals, beliefs, morality, discipline, revolutionary standpoint, interpersonal relations, and so on." Furthermore, Jiang Zemin attached great importance to the construction of Spiritual

On June 13th, 2014, the activity of "socialist core values" in photos was held at Xidan Culture Plaza in Beijing, describing China Dream by photos.

Civilization, arming people with scientific theory, guiding people with the correct consensus, shaping people with the lofty ideals, inspiring people with outstanding works, carrying forward the theme of the times, and promoting diversity. In 2001, he proposed combining "rule by virtue" with "rule by law", strengthening the role of moral construction in the entire national development.

Furthermore, the 16th CPC National Congress report proposed a new task: "to establish a socialist ideological and ethical system in harmony with the socialist market economy, socialist legal norms, and the traditional Chinese virtues". In February of 2004, the CPC Central Committee and State Council issued *Opinions on Further Strengthening and Improving the Ideological and Moral Construction of Minors*, thus launching a campaign to maintain advanced education activity in the party members and cadres, thereby strengthening the ideological and moral construction. In March of 2006, Hu Jintao put forward and elaborated "Eight Honors and Eight Disgraces"[1] In October, the Sixth

On June 5th, 2014, Luo Laiqing, a folk artist was showing the manuscript and sculpture copy expressing "justice" and "law" in socialist core values.

Ideology Construction

Plenary Session of the 16th CPC expounded the task of building a socialist core value system, of which the main contents include guiding ideology of Marxism, the common ideal of socialism with Chinese characteristics, national spirit with patriotism as the core, the spirit of the times with reform and innovation as the core, and Socialist Concept of Honor and Disgrace. In the October of 2011, the "Decision" issued on the Sixth Plenary Session of the 17th CPC National Congress elaborated "how to promote the construction of socialist core value system" in a special section of the document.

In the November of 2012, The 16th CPC National Congress formally initiated the goal of cultivating and practicing the socialist core values: prosperity, democracy, civilization, harmony, freedom, equality, justice, the rule of law, patriotism, dedication, integrity, and kindness. These words are highly condensed and concentrated into the main expression of the socialist core value system.

Socialist core values determine the basic standards of the values system. Achieving prosperity, democracy, civilization and harmony is the value goal from the perspective of the nation. This is also the basic value standard for the national economic, political, cultural, social and ecological civilization construction. In addition, it is China's goal of building a modern socialist country, reflecting the fundamental requirement of China's development since the dawn of the modern era. Being the appeal to core values after trying to achieve economic development, political civilization, cultural prosperity, and social progress, this goal also unifies the nation's development goal and value goal.

Achieving freedom, equality, justice and the rule of law is the value goal from the perspective of the society. This is the basic value standard for Chinese society's comprehensive development and progress and is the value requirements towards social systems and rules. Marx and Engels once stated that "the free development of each person" and "the free development of all" is

Contemporary China's Culture

On December 21st, 2010, "National Moral Model Story-telling Session" grassroots tour went to Huairou District in Beijing. The tour was co-held by Central Civilization Office and China Federation of Literary and Art Circles and other institutions, spreading good deeds by talking and singing arts.

a sign of a new society. Freedom, equality, and justice are essential attributes and intrinsic requirements of socialism, and the rule of law is a fundamental safeguard to ensure the orderly operation of the society.

Achieving patriotism, dedication, integrity, and kindness is the value goal from the perspective of the individual level, which is the basic moral norms that citizen should abide by and is also the value standard for people's national identity, individual virtues, professional ethics and interpersonal communication. This standard is not only the modernization of Chinese traditional virtues, but also integrates the moral essence of CPC revolution and the new socialist era.

The socialist core values incorporate both the excellent Chinese traditional culture and the best achievements of human civilization. While, the

Ideology Construction

structure of traditional Chinese culture values is diverse, the Confucian values constitute the mainstream values of the Chinese civilization. The Confucian ethical views include benevolence, righteousness, propriety, wisdom, and faith. Out of all of these listed values, the core value is benevolence, caring for oneself as well as others. Being kindhearted and people-oriented, being faithful and righteous, worshiping harmony and seeking common ground are important values of Confucianism. Governance of social order should depend on morals for self-discipline and depend on the rule of law for heteronomy, with the "Confucian virtue" as the core. This provides both strong cohesion, and tremendous assimilation force for the Chinese nation, which is an important reason why China has a long history and strong vitality. Under the guidance of Confucianism, China's attitude towards the outside world advocates good-neighborliness, and explicitly does not advocate expanding the national territory, as well as advocates against violence.

On March 18th, 2014, a teacher was introducing the 24-word "socialist core values" to the students at Huanfeng Primary School in Hanshan County, Anhui Province.

The Chinese people attach great importance to blood ties and family values, but it is stressed that the nation is one big family and keeping this big family as the primary priority is a very important part of traditional Chinese culture. Chinese classics recorded that King Yu passed his home three times without entering while combating a major flood, which is a good example to show that he values the "big family" (his nation) more than his own small family. Mencius said, the gentleman should "be courageous enough to shoulder responsibilities"; which means that they should take the world affairs as their own responsibility. In the modern times, the Sino-Japanese War greatly enhanced the Chinese people's love for their own country and gave the nation's population the modern sense of patriotism. In this way the concept of "the unification of small family and big family" gradually came into being. Especially during the period of Anti-Japanese War, the Chinese people suffered tremendous pain at the hands of the foreign invaders. A new solemnness of self-reliance and national rejuvenation was added to this concept. Furthermore, the people took the initiative to combine their own fate with the national fate. The Chinese people are profoundly aware of that only once we are united together, will the country be filled with hope. Socialist core values are a perfect combination of traditional Chinese values and the new elements that exist in accordance with the current situation. The country's political ideals and social values that are embodied by socialist core values are all perfectly integrated with personal ethic codes, which take some references from Confucianism.

Socialist core values also take some reference from capitalist civilization, making whose best achievements "freedom, democracy, equality" the basic contents of socialist value system, reflecting the compatibility of socialist core values. It's worth mentioning that socialist core values absorbed this reasonable and positive content of Capitalist civilization and overcame the individualism, money worship, hedonism, and other negative tendencies that plague the western capitalist societies.

In conclusion, Socialist core values have unified the history, reality, western society and future, embodied the internal unification of nation, society and individual, and showed its unique value.

Cultivating and Practicing Socialist Core Values

The fact that China has proposed cultivating and practicing the socialist core values is based on the current situation in the nation. Under the condition of reform and Opening-up and development of the socialist market economy, ideology is characterized by multiple diversities. Values conflicts amongst individuals, groups, and different social subjects are reflected in the fact that they have different or even opposite perspectives in terms of efficiency and fairness, interests and moral values, freedom and equality and a series of other important issues. Different forms of values also have some contradictions and conflicts, for example, the tradition against the modern, the local against the foreign, the religious against the secular, and the elite against the mass. Profit-driven market economy has triggered money worship, consumerism and hedonism in the society, resulting in some people losing faith, worshipping nihilism, anxious, indifferent, regardless of right and wrong, beauty and ugliness, shame and grace. These problems also find many manifestations in our real lives: the moral bottom line frequently falls backward, the laggard feudal superstition floats up again, extreme religious thought came up; a variety of kitsch and vulgar culture becomes popular, and some evil people unscrupulously tamper with the history of the people and the nation. The coexistence of the lofty and the selfish, the co-existence of advanced and backward culture, and the commensalism of the positive and negative culture reflect that the value appeal of the masses is in chaos.

For the sake of development, China needs to establish core values, improve the system of values and propel the value goal of governance, thus boosting people's sense of value judgment and moral responsibility. Once this

Ideology Construction

happens, the people will be able to distinguish what is good and beautiful, what is evil and ugly. Meanwhile, this value should be able to gather people from different classes and education backgrounds to work together and seek common points while reserving difference. In the November of 2013, the 18th Plenary Session of the CPC Central Committee issued *On Deepening Reform*

Post of movie "*Young Leifeng*".

of Certain Major Issue Decision, proposing to cultivate and practice the socialist core values, put it into the whole process of national education, and put it into practice when it comes to the economic development practice and social governance. In addition, the publicity and education about these values is also of great significance.

In order to make it easier to follow and practice such values, socialist core values are to be formed at different value-oriented levels. To cultivate and practice the socialist core values, it should first be implemented in the socialist economic development and social governance practices, paying special attention to policy support and forming a system guarantee that could help combine the values with people's life. The second requirement is the unification of theoretical knowledge and practice. Knowledge is both the prerequisite and foundation, because only inner recognition will lead to final conscious practice. Therefore, publicity and education is a basic work that should be included in the whole process of national education. The "Decision" demands integrity, social morality, professional ethics, family virtues and personal moral education, guiding people to pursue ethical and moral life. So that all the 1.3 billion Chinese people will behave well and spread the virtue and Chinese culture. In this way, cultivating and practicing socialist core values becomes a process of shaping and cultivating people.

The Central Committee of the CPC requires the Party members and cadres set a good example and act as social role model by being self-disciplined, well-conducted, caring, pragmatic, honest and upright. At the same time, the education and supervision for the Party members and cadres is to be strengthened, especially the leading cadres, for the violation of law will be investigated very strictly. So if they are corrupt, do or have done immoral things, or evaded responsibility, they will be severely punished.

The use of the Party as a role model is an important way to cultivate and practice the socialist core values to encourage the good and demonstrate the

Ideology Construction

On November 9th, 2013, student volunteers in Liaocheng University, Shandong Province are making paper cuts to celebrate the opening of the Third Plenary Session of the 18th Central Committee of the Chinese Communist Party.

typical. "Learn from Comrade Lei Feng" has been an example of following a role model for decades. Since the new century, the Chinese government not only commended the science and technology experts who conducted significant inventions, but also honored those unknown devotees with ordinary jobs. In the October of 2002, CCTV launched an activity to elect the most outstanding devotees, of which the theme is "Moving China". People elected in this year include excellent scientists and entrepreneurs, as well as "folk heroes, such as Alimu who did charity by selling roasted mutton and Meng Peijie who took good care of his foster mother for more than 12 years.

There is a singer from Shenzhen named Cong Fei among the "Moving China figures" in 2005. During 11 years, he adhered to donate to the dropout students and the disabled in Sichuan, Guizhou, and other impoverished mountainous areas while doing volunteering work. Furthermore, in 2006, he decided to donate his corneas before he died due to illness later that year. After Cong Fei died, thousands of people went to see him off. The people

Contemporary China's Culture

On January 15th, 2006, at the award ceremony of CCTV's *Touching the Heart of China - Person of the Year 2005*, young singer Congfei was elected.

in Shenzhen acted in the memory of such a noble soul: a Shenzhen Youth Foundation named "Cong Fei student special fund" was established, not only to help more children to go to school, but also to take care of his children. Now, Shenzhen has 846,000 registered volunteers.

Recent years have seen people are looking for "the most beautiful people" around. There are the most beautiful teacher, the most beautiful fighter, the most beautiful mother, the most beautiful police person, the most beautiful nurse, the most beautiful bride and so on. These civilian heroes' unyielding pursuit of the good and the beautiful exerts a strong reaction in the community, making people realize that the "good guys are all around us", adding their own confidence in their ability to reshape social morality.

In addition, the central media also carried out a large-scale public benefit activity to find "the most beautiful village doctor", "the most beautiful village teacher", and "the most beautiful village official", and dedicated itself to

Ideology Construction

On June 11th, 2012, large public service activity "Finding the Most Beautiful Country Teacher" co-organized by CCTV and Guang Ming Daily was officially launched at Media Center Hotel in Beijing.

writing down the stories of those whom are working under the most difficult environment and conditions while making selfless and silent contribution to society. These stories demonstrate the social mainstream values and boost people's positive attitude and the sense of social responsibility, thus creating a positive energy for the masses during the period of social transition.

In the September of 2013, the fourth session of national moral model selection results were announced, the CPC Central Committee General Secretary Xi Jinping met with 54 national moral models and 265 nominees. The country allocated 3 million special funds to 34 low-income and poor moral models, helping deliver the country's value orientation, boosting the formation of public order and civilized fashion.

As a big socialist developing country, China is striding forward to become a modern socialist country. At this moment, it is quite necessary to actively cultivate and practice the socialist core values, guiding people correctly understand the future and destiny of the nation, accumulate the cohesion and mental strength, punish the evil and promote the good, cultivating people's correct moral judgment, moral responsibility and a benevolence-centered civilized morality. As the Reformation ideologist Martin Luther said: "the prosperity of a country doesn't lie on the well-off national treasury, sturdy castle or public facilities, it lies on the people's civilization accomplishment, which means their education, vision and noble character." Chinese famous modern thinker and writer Lu Xun once said: "the most precious thing for a country is the soul of this nation. Only when it was carried forward, will Chinese people really progress."

Explanation

1. Eight Honors, Eight Disgraces:

    Love the country; do it no harm.

    Serve the people; do no disservice.

    Follow science; discard ignorance.

    Be diligent; not indolent.

    Be united, help each other; make no gains at other's expense.

    Be honest and trustworthy; do not spend ethics for profits.

    Live plainly, struggle hard; do not wallow in luxuries and pleasures.

Literature & Art Flourish Together

Contemporary Chinese literature and art grow in step with the evolution of Contemporary society. As a result of the recent economic prosperity of the country, literature and art thrive as never before. This growth of the arts is reflected in the following ways: the rapidly increasing number of compositions, increasingly rich expression techniques, and growing influence of art works. Each personalized art work is the epitome of civilization of a great age. In the development of the both literature and art, the novel is the main force in literature and in turn, literature forms the key component of art. Contemporary Chinese literature is very abundant and the emerging network of literature continues to develop rapidly. Moreover, film creation prospers and stage art continuously offers new works to the citizens of the People's Republic of China.

Literary Creation Is in Full Swing, Network Literature Develops Rapidly

China's literary world is rich in talents and there is a group of diligent writers brave enough to learn and explore. Since the new century, the group has been expanding and literary creation is unprecedentedly active. Some of the Chinese writers active in contemporary literary world include Wang Meng, Zhang Jie born in the 1930s and Han Han, Zhang Yueran and Guo Jingming born in the 1980s. Today, about six generations of authors are writing, which may be called "six generations live under one roof". Some writers born in the 1950s and 1960s marched into the literary world and took a pioneer role in the 1980s such as Mo Yan, Jia Pingao, Zhang Wei, Yan Lianke, Liu Zhenyun,

On November 10th, 2005, Scholarly Festival of the South was opened in Flower City Exhibition Center in Guangzhou.

Three Literature & Art Flourish Togethe

On December 14th, 2012, Mo Yan (in the middle) was warmly welcomed at Beijing Capital International Airport after he won the Nobel Prize in Literature.

Tie Ning, Wang Anyi, Han Shaogong, Zhang Chengzhi, Su Tong, Yu Hua, Ge Fei. They remain the main force in the literary world. As the most influential writers, they pay close attention to the livelihood of the people and the society and each author has their own distinctive language art style. Such newly emerging talent writers as Han Han, Guo Jingming, Xu Zechen, Sheng Keyi, Di An, Yan Ge born in the 1970s and 1980s are the most active writers in modern literary creation circle of China. Their life experiences, courses and values were generated with the development of China's market economy and their compositions and publications cater to their peers' tastes, which brings fresh experience and achievement to contemporary literature. The ranks of ethnic group writers are continuously growing. Now all 55 ethnic groups are represented in the Chinese Writers Association, a number that accounts for 13% of the total. They produce many excellent works as well.

In the present Chinese literary creation, works are both abundant and cover a variety of subjects. Among them, long novel has developed rapidly and

Contemporary China's Culture

enjoys a place of prominence. Since entering the new century, long novels are produced with an average of 1000 annually, especially after the year of 2008. The number of published long novels reached 4300 in 2011, making China one of the top novel publishing nations in the world. Many long novels are set in rural China and historical narratives. Representative works include Mo Yan's *Frog*, Chen Zhongshi's *White Deer Plain*, Jia Pingao's *Shaanxi Opera*, Alai's *The Dust Settled*, Bi Feiyu's *the Plain*, Zhou Meisen's *The Public Prosecution* and Lu Tianming's *Gao Wei Du Zhan Li* which vividly depict the process of China's reform and Opening-up; Wang Meng's *Awkward and Romantic* demonstrates a history of intellectual spiritual course. Chi Zijian's *On the Right Bank of Arguna River* and Alai's *Zhan Dui* reflect ethnic groups' vicissitudes of history and national spirits. Such works as Yu Hua's *Brothers*, Dong Xi's *Regret*, Wang Anyi's *Heroes Everywhere* and Bi Feiyu's *Massage* present a great society through the lives of the little people. Moreover, some excellent long novels like Tie Ning's *Stupid Flower*, Mo Yan's *Fatigues of Life and Death*, Shi Tiesheng's *My Journey of Dingyi*, Fan Wen's *Grief Earth*, Liu Qingbang's *Red Coal*, and animal culture novels as Jiang Rong's *Wolf Totem* and Yang Zhijun's *Tibetan Mastiffs* represent the Chinese literary creation achievements and the artistic standards in the new century.

In the field of documentary literature, some works like He Jianming's *The Country—Unprecedented Action in the Diplomatic History of China*, Fang Fang's *Wuchang City*, Chen Qiwen's *Beijing Storm*, Ye Duoduo's *A Person's Dianchi Battle* are masterpieces of reportage in recent years. Meanwhile, in biographical literature, quite a few works analyze the depth and strength of historical destiny through some characters' fate, which is a significant breakthrough compared to the past. In the aspect of proses and essays, proses from the perspective of history and culture are flourishing, represented by Feng Jicai, Sun Yu, Han Xiaohui, Xu Gang, etc. Besides, ecological proses describing natural variations and environmental problems gradually prevail, drawing the attention of many people.

Three Literature & Art Flourish Togethe

Cover of novel *The Wolf Totem.*

The following figures help to map the current development status of Chinese literature: there are more than 900 literary journals and about 1000 collection of essays published annually, showing a prosperous literature scene. The novel *Shaanxi Opera* sold more than 200,000 copies in less than one month after it was published. In 2013, *Children's Literature* celebrated it's fiftieth anniversary by issuing over one million copies monthly and it has become an important part of many children's lives. Among the ranking list of top ten books across the world given by the United Nations in 2011, *Pi Pi Lu* written by Zheng Yuanjie, a famous writer of children's literature, and *Harry Potter* written by an English author JK Rowling were tied for fourth. Yang Hongying, another writer of children's literature, has a total of 87 works in her more than 30 years' writing life and sold more than 60 million copies.

Contemporary China's Culture

In 2012, Mo Yan won the Nobel Prize for literature, which is an iconic event indicating Chinese literature prominence around the world. "The Red Sorghum" series written by Mo Yan in the mid 1980s are called a mixed chorus between tough folkway and national righteousness and have been sold worldwide and translated into over 20 languages. In the new century, after experiencing both pioneering and aboriginality, as well as both experimental and nationalization, he constantly surpasses himself and continues to write a large number of medium-length novels and short stories and excellent long novels like *Big Breasts & Wide Hips*, *White Sandalwood Punishment*, *Fatigues of Life and Death* and *Frog* based on encompassing both foreign literature resources and native literary traditions. *Frog* won the top honor prize of Chinese literary—the 8th Mao Dun Literature Awards. The primary reason why Mo Yan was awarded the Nobel Prize for Literature is that he blends folktales, history, and modern society through illusion realism. The prize is a recognition and praise for his outstanding literary achievements, and it is also

On April 20th, 2014, Yang Hongying (2nd right) was communicating with her little readers at Xinhua Bookstore in Jimo, Shandong Province.

Three Literature & Art Flourish Togethe

an affirmation of the world for Chinese contemporary literature. The prize certainly will attract much more attention to Chinese literary across the world.

Since the 1990s, with the gradually rise of marketization of China's economy, as well as the technicalization of information, popularization of culture, entertainment trend of media; a new structure of "one divides into three" appeared in the development of literature. This concept is defined as conventional literature taking literary journals as its base to continue to develop in prospect, the marketization of literature (or mass literature) by adopting the means of market operation, and lastly, network media-based new media literature that strongly reproduces in polarization. Since then, an unprecedented complex and complicated situation in literature has appeared.

Even though it has only been a dozen years since the emerging network

Cover of Mo Yan's work *The Frog*.

literature appeared in the late 20th century, it has developed very rapidly. The total number of such works has grown quickly with large stock and various types. It attracts extensive readership as well as multitude writers. All these have made it the largest literature group in the current Chinese literary world. Poetry writing, a form of literature that once appeared doomed, lives again in the way of "network poetry" and "work poetry". Up to the end of December of 2012, there were over 500 frequently updated literature websites and the number of people who published works on the internet in different ways is over 20 million among which there were 2 million registered network writers. These registered writers broke literary genre boundaries and devoted themselves to cross-style writing which usually appeared in the form of typed such as online game novels, urban life novels, time-travel novels, mystery novels, fantasy novels and so on. The number of literature netizens is now 274 million, which has developed into universal literature in some sense. From May to October in 2013, 23 domestic large internet firms jointly hosted "2013 Internet Culture

On October 28th, 2008, the activity of "Ten Years Inventory of Network Literature" led by Chinese Writers Association was started in Beijing, which is the first barrier-breaking meeting of entity creators and electric creators.

Season" and have launched Network Novel and Short Stories Competition and Micronovels competition. A total of 300,000 works contributed to an original website owned by Shengda Literature, among which 120 excellent works were picked out and received more than 100 million views.

Network literature is rapidly growing into a powerful force which cannot be ignored from a form of network writers' own enjoyment. At present, there are more than 30,000 authors who keep writing on web platforms and live on remuneration. The number of people employed in the network writing equals the number of professional and semiprofessional writers in the system. From the point of writing trend, the boundary between a part of network literature and traditional literature on the subject, content and style faded with each passing day. Some of the network literature has been gradually accepted by traditional literature world and some works even have been adapted for TV series in which the most successful examples are *Legend of Concubine Zhen Huan*, *Du Lala's Promotion Story* and *Step by Step*. Moreover, sixteen network writers were selected to 2013 Development Member List of CWA announced by Chinese Writers' Association. Network literature has become the main components of popular literature in a nonprofessional writing exercise and basic trend of continuously tilting to categorization.

However, in terms of the quality of network literature, the good and the bad are intermingled. Traditional literature still plays a leading role. Emphasis has been put on the contacts and trainings of new network literary authors by Writers' Associations and Literary Federations across the country. These new network authors have been regarded as the reserve forces for literary writing. In October 2013, Chinese Literature Association helped establish a university of non-profit network literature and provided free training for network literature authors across the country with the objective of training 100,000 people per year. The author Mo Yan served as honorary president of the university.

Contemporary China's Culture

The challenges facing Chinese Literary in the new century are as follows: with the accelerated pace of commercialization of the literature, popularization has become a popular culture trend resulting in superficial thoughts of many literary works and a lack of artistic quality. People realized writers must stick to the soul of the literature, go deeper to into the stream of life and dive into the hearts of humans to reflect the reality of our times and improve the internal quality of the literature so that a great atmosphere in Chinese literature can take shape.

Growing Film Appeal in China

More than 100 years ago, Chinese people combined traditional opera culture and new film technology ingeniously and created special "shadow play" film, which was the birth of Chinese film. By the 1970s, film is a popular mass culture and reached an audience of 29.3 billion per year and with an average of 28 times per capita.

The current Chinese film creation features multi-products, multi-types and diversification. Chinese film first started to implement market-oriented reform in an all-round way, which further stimulated creative vitality. Currently, the leading figure is the fifth generation directors who grew up in the mid-1980s and created the new ear of Chinese film such as Zhang Yimou, Chen Kaige, Feng Xiaogang etc.

Zhang Yimou is famous for *Red Sorghum*, a work that absorbs nutrition from the soil of local culture and learns from foreign experience and the lessons of advanced film. Unconstrained imagination, a fantasy story, an all-star cast and beautifully choreographed action sequences attracted large audiences. The film also received several awards at the International Film Festival. *Raise the Red Lantern, Ju Dou,* and *Hero* directed by Zhang Yimou were nominated for Best Foreign Language Film in the Academy Awards. Moreover, *Soundtracks for Shanghai Triad, House of Flying Daggers* and *Curse of the Golden Flowe*r were nominated for best cinematography and Best Costume Design in the Academy Awards. Zhang has become China's most influential filmmaker in the international film circle. He also successfully choreographed the opening ceremony for 2008 Summer Olympics in Beijing which amazed the world by the beauty of the art and culture. His film, *Under the Hawthorn Tree* in 2010 recovering one's original simplicity depicted an innocent and undying

A poster of the film *The Story of Qiu Ju* directed by Zhang Yimou.

love which is sincere. It was the first movie performances for both the hero and heroine. It also received the highest ticket sales of any Chinese romantic movie.

Feng Xiaogang pioneered New Year's greeting films in the Chinese mainland. He has a good understanding of Chinese audience's life interest and present daily experience so as to pursue the touching story which operates at a lower cost for domestic audiences' positive reaction. Such films as *The Two Parties, Big Shots, Cell Phone, A World without Thieves, If You Are the One* directed by Feng highlight social problems in comedic form and make people appreciate open-minded life with laughter through self-ridiculed humorous languages, optimistic life attitudes, special warmth and sentimentalism caused by populace tendency. In recent years, Feng has tried to outperform himself. He produced *the Banquet* and *Assembly* combing the charm of "warmth" and "sentimentalism" story accepted by the public with highly contagious audio-visual effects of blockbusters which brought more diversified appearance to Chinese blockbusters. Moreover, Feng also directed *Back to 1942* with dignified style which was based on Liu Zhenyun's novel *Remembering 1942*.

Chen Kaige is adept at analyzing how human's spirit is restricted and influenced by the burden of tradition and history to express strong humane consciousness and aesthetic pursuit with his profound cultural foundation and solid art skill. Besides, he mobilizes a variety of filming methods and developed a unique movie style heavy featuring heavy and sharp, peace and agitation. The films he has directed include culture movies such as *Yellow Earth, Farewell My Concubine*, and *Mei Lanfang*. Recently Chen also directed a movie called *Caught in the Web* paying attention to status and changes of all kinds of people through the violence of the conscience and described struggle between good and evil in the mind.

The spirit of realistic creation is the tradition and artistic character of

Post of movie *So Young*.

Chinese film. The changing great stage deeply attracts contemporary art creator. In recent years, a lot of Chinese filmmakers have made a self-conscious attempt at realistic writing techniques. From *Love Is Not Blind, the Piano in A Factory, A Simple Life* to *Finding Mr Right, So Young* and *American Dreams in China*, although their subjects and expressive methods are different and film style changes from realism, mystery to criticism, they all focus their cameras on ordinary people's life and realistic difficulties in the transition to observe an individual's fate with warm eyes. This reveals the struggle of human nature and expresses humanistic concern. The re-emergence of realistic spirits contributes to reversing the tendency of being too commercial reflected by entertainment first, behind-closed-doors, and simple imitations.

China's "Fifth-generation" directors have created brilliant achievements in Chinese film and have sent some films with Chinese characteristics into international film stage. In recent years, a new generation of directors, represented by Jia Zhangke and Lu Chuan, is also emerging. These directors dare to innovate and make new breakthroughs in art technique, which has exerted great influence in international film circle. *Xiao Wu, platform, Unknown Pleasures, The World* and *Still life* directed by Jia Zhangke have shown the people's daily life in China since 1990. *Xiao Wu*, his first feature film, received good recommendations from *Cahiers Du Cinema* in French. In 2006, his film *Still life* won the Golden Lion award at the Venice International Film Festival and the Best Foreign-language Film award at the Los Angeles Film Critics Association (LAFCA) awards. Jia was also awarded Golden Leopard of life achievement by Locarno International Film Festival in 2010 which made him the youngest filmmaker to receive this honor. Jia said "I try to care about average people through film, and then first I should respect mundane life. So you can feel joy and heaviness of every plain life as time passes slowly."

The Missing Gun wrote by Lu Chuan in 2012 is also his debut film and got exposure in the film circle. Later, *Ke Ke Xi Li* and *City of Life And Death*

Three Literature & Art Flourish Togethe

Jia Zhangke, one of the sixth-generation directors won the Gold Lion for Best Film by his work *Still Life* on the 63rd Venice Film Festival.

directed by Lu have won several domestic and international awards.

A batch of cross-sector directors of the young generation show great potential. Xu Jinglei became the first one trying to direct as well as perform as an excellent actress. *My Father and I* was a film that was self-wrote, self-directed and self-performed by her and won best directorial debut at 23th Golden Rooster Awards with an investment of only 2 million RMB. After that, she directed a series of movies such as *Cherish Our Love Forever, Letter from a Strange Woman*, and *Go Lala Go*. Actor Xu Zheng and Actress Zhao Wei directed *Lost in Thailand* and *So Young* respectively. Zhao Xiaolu, the director of *Finding Mr Right* is a teacher of the Department of Beijing Film Academy literature. Wu Ershan, the director of *Painted Skin* 2 was famous for advertisements before making his film debut.

Chinese film with constant boom and development draws the attention to the whole world. In 2011, a total of 295 Chinese films attended 82 Film Festivals in 28 nations and Hong Kong, Macao and Taiwan regions, among which 55 films won 82 awards in 18 Film Festivals.

Behind the situation of rapid development of Chinese film in terms of quantity and the box office, there also exist many inadequacies and deficiencies in creation. Recent years some technologies for big-budget movies have approached the international level, but serious exploratory movies have not been taken up. The film artistic standards still need to be improved in areas such as roughens of film language and homogenization of the story.

In recent years, Chinese TV series have a powerful vitality that is reflected by a broad array of topics, a wide variety of styles and continually updated form. The representative works include *Braving the Journey to the Northeast, Bright Sword, Soldiers Sortie, Long March, Lurk, Golden Marriage, and the Iron Age*. Some TV series like *Legend of Bruce Lee and Legend of Concubine Zhen Huan* have also been broadcasted on American television.

New Works in Stage Art Continuously Released

Chinese opera is a representative art with national characteristic features and tradition in Chinese performing arts. Lifestyle change and cultural entertainment's diversification caused by China's Economic Transition have put stage art in a depressed state. In 2002, Wei Minglun, a famous playwright, triggered a discussion on the fate of Chinese opera. In order to save stage art, the Ministry of Finance and the Ministry of Culture took this opportunity to jointly implement a quality project for national stage art aiming at supporting the development of stage art. Special funds in annual investment supported the production of high-quality works as well as promoted the cooperation between

On August 28th, *Dujiangyan—Time Travel*, a super multimedia dream play made its first official debut in Dujiangyan, Sichuan Province. It is a combination of acrobatics, dancing, drama, music and multimedia technology of world first class.

cultural troupes and outside world in talents, capital, play planning, and marketing so as to effectively integrate resources and expand the market.

Excellent projects of national stage art have established a performance promotion mechanism; the purpose of which was to facilitate cultural exchanges and marketing through drama performances, shows and watching competition. There were 119 plays that participated in the 2012 national excellent drama performance. Art category covered some major categories like traditional operas, modern dramas, children's dramas, operas, ballet, song and dance poems, and musicals. Except Peking Opera and Kun Opera, traditional operas also covered some local dramas like Pingju Opera, Hebei Clapper Opera, Henan Opera, Shanxi Opera, Shaoxing Opera, Shanghai Opera, Sichuan Opera, shaanxi Opera. Participating operas covered a wide range of subjects including realistic subjects praising heroes and reflecting ordinary people's lives, traditional operas' collection and adaptation and new history operas. All of these operas pay considerable attention to the innovation of stage performance forms and advanced stage technology so as to constantly enrich and improve artistic appeal and expression force of the works. Chinese Peking Opera Theatre and Tibetan Operas Troupe jointly organized the rehearsal of *Wencheng Princess* through cross-region and art varieties' cooperation. An integration of Tibetan Opera with Beijing Opera mobilizing opera art noumenon means was a new exploration of the artistic form. Shanghai Media Group, China Performing Art Agency, Shanghai Acrobatic Troupe and Shanghai Circus City combined the resources of news media, performances overseas, and performers with performance places co-creating acrobatics *Chrono Trigger*. *Swan Lake* was also a similar artistic attempt. These operas integrated arts like acrobatics, dance and opera together resulting in good stage effects which gave people refreshing artistic feelings.

Since 2010, the Ministry of Culture has organized excellent drama performances of national art troupes consecutively to promote artistic innovation, realize "the modernization of traditional art" and "the nationalization of foreign art" and cultivate young and middle-aged talents in the arts. There were 32 performances in 2010 and 36 performances in 2011, among which there were 18 newly created plays which account for 50%. Among 35 performances in 2012, there were 23 newly created plays which account for two thirds of participating operas. Some awards and titles issued by the state like Art Festival Grand Prize, Wenhua Grand Prize, "National Five Top Project Award" and the title of excellent plays of national stage art guided and promoted the creation of excellent dramas.

Peking Opera is the country's national opera. The Ministry of Culture and the Ministry of Finance enacted *Protect and Support Plan for National Key Peking Opera Troupes*. Central government invested 50 million RMB of special funds from 2006 to 2010. From 2011 onwards, the plan entered into the second stage and there is 10 million RMB invested in it annually to support national key Peking Opera troupes.

On November 4th, 2012 Beijing Small Hundred Flower Yue Opera Troupe was giving their performance at Cultural Center in Xicheng District.

Theater arts creation has received strong government support in the last dozen years. National Endowment for the Arts was founded in June 2013 which would support the development of excellent dramas through project subsidies, rewarding excellence and matching funds. Under the supports of local governments and the efforts of folk art workers, some local arts like the northeast song-and-dance duet, story-telling and ballad singing in Suzhou dialect, Changde Gushu, Weizhou Guzici, Northern Shaanxi storytelling and Henan Zhuizi maintained fresh condition and showed a state of favorable development.

In addition, the government has vigorously advocated returning the drama to citizens. First, the government encourages that drama subjects should be close to citizens. Realistic subject dramas have paid more attention to ordinary people's life and bring the drama back to market by ordinary people's perspective and modern aesthetic. Second, the government encourages privately operated drama. According to the Chinese Ballad Singers Association, there are more than 3000 private folk art groups and more than 70 state-owned folk art groups, together employing more than 250,000 people across the country. Some brand private drama troupes have appeared, such as Lin Zhaohua Drama Studio. Local drama troupes are flourishing. There are hundreds of private Yueju Opera troupes in Zhejiang province. The Chinese Folk Azalea Drama Festival is held every two years to provide a platform for private troupes to perform and communicate. Some folk spontaneous theatergoers troupes, working at ordinary times and acting in their free time, direct and act all by themselves, and recreate by themselves. Students' drama activities are lively, and in the professional and amateur student's drama club, members are not only the basic audience but also the reserve forces of the drama.

The Chinese drama production has experienced a trend of multiplex symbiosis. Little theatre dramas that began in the 1980s are now welcomed by the market. Some influential experimental theater dramas have entered the grand theatre to perform, and participated in the national awards selection of the Cao Yu Drama Award. Meanwhile, the variety has spread from drama to Peking Opera, operas, Shanghai opera and Kunqu Opera, etc. The short preparation period and lower cost of small theater plays have allowed it to become an important dimension in drama production. In places such as Beijing, Shanghai, the "white collar drama" which factually reflects the urban white-collars' life. The white-collar drama has attracted many white-collar workers and has become a unique art form.

The exploration of Chinese avant-garde opera is compelling, and the representative figure is Meng Jinghui. In 2007, the modern drama *Life Opinions of Two Dogs* directed by Meng Jinghui was performed. Observing the world from the perspective of "dogs", the drama complained social quirk in a humorous and ironic way, brought joy and reflection to audiences and delivered an optimistic life attitude. The form of this drama is still a novelty. Improvisation and realism performance are integrated together and two actors

On May 5th, 2007, *"Life Opinions of Two Dogs"*, a modern drama directed by Meng Jinghui was played at Pioneer Theater.

Contemporary China's Culture

On the night of June 18th, 2012, Muslim dance drama *The Moon Over the Helan Mountain* was played at Mei Lanfang Theater in Beijing, in which it praised the harmony and peaceful development between different nationalities and cultures.

play more than 30 characters in two hours and led audiences to taste varied and complex life in a relaxed and humorous atmosphere. By November 2013, the modern drama has been performed a total of 1000 times in 6 years in 30 cities of China, the Kennedy art center in Washington and British Edinburgh international festival. The modern drama *Alive* based on a same name work written by Yu Hua, directed by Meng Jinghui has also been very successful and is considered as a dual success model of art and commerce.

Since the new century, there is a significant amount of Chinese dance dramas. In recent years, many excellent Chinese dance dramas have been created, such as *Red River Valley, Thousand-arm Kwan-yin, Beautiful Sunset, Raise the Red Lantern, The Moon over the Helan Mountain*, and *The Peacock*. The grand musical and dance epic *The Road to Rejuvenation* has been performed 100 times and more than 200,000 audiences have watched the live show. The dance drama which premiered in January 2007, *The Moon over the Helan Mountain,* was a grand dance drama and the first to reflect the history and folk custom of the Hui nationality in a panoramic view. The story was a legendary and touching love story between the Muslim caravans and the people under the Helan Mountain on the ancient Silk Road. The grand magnificent dancing scene reflected the harmony of the nation, as well as the blending and developing history between Islamic and Chinese civilization. In this dance drama, the main part was the ethnic and folk dance in northwest and Arab dance, integrating modern dance and ballet elements, reflecting the regional cultural symbols through the stage background and props. It was not only performed more than 430 shows domestically, but also repeatedly went to Egypt, Qatar, Algeria and other Arab countries, and became China's "culture card" of foreign exchange.

In the aspect of dance, Yang Liping, the folk dancer, was famous for self-complied dance *Spirit of the Peacock* both at home and abroad in the 1980s. *The Moonlight, Two Trees, Qomolangma* and *Lhasa River* are her major works. In 2003, Yang Liping created a large natural dance drama *Dynamic Yunnan* that integrated the essence of native local songs and dances and classical folk dance and combined traditional and modern beauty with high artistry and ornamental value. In 2009, *The Sound of Yunnan*, directed and starred by Yang, was successful again. In 2012, the multi-ethnic and natural dance drama *The Peacock* created and starred by Yang, centering on two eternal themes of life and love, delivered artists' thinking and feeling for art and life to the audiences, expressing the original pursuit of freedom and life. In this dance drama, the native and pristine folk song and dance contrasted to new artistic conception, using color to show the turn of spring, summer, autumn and winter. Therefore, it became the most popular dance drama of China in 2013.

Cultural Construction

The cultural construction driven by the Chinese government is focused on basic cultural undertakings, including establishing a system of public cultural services, ensuring people's fundamental cultural rights and interests and satisfying people's basic cultural needs. Meanwhile, it also includes the protection of cultural heritage and Chinese civilization, standardization of Mandarin Chinese and its protection as a national language.

The Construction of the Basic Framework of a Public Cultural Service System

According to the rules of non-profit, fairness, public welfare and convenience, China's public cultural service system is government-led, supported by public finances and people-oriented. The non-profit cultural institutions have been set up as the backbone of this system focused on the grass-roots, especially rural areas and central and western regions. The government is devoted to meeting the needs of people's basic cultural rights and interests or culture, including the right to read books and newspapers, listening to the radio and watching television, public cultural appreciation and participation in public cultural activities, and more.

There are two main kinds of cultural institutions in China. The first kind is national nonprofit cultural institutions such as museums, libraries, science and technology museums, public arts gallery and other similar institutions. A second kind is the publishing units responsible for political and public welfare such as radio and television, news agencies, current politics, communist party newspaper, the key social science research institutions and artistic troupes of ethnic and national level, and so on.

The Chinese government has long promoted the construction of a public cultural service system as part of a reform of the country's cultural system. Based on the principles of convenience, fundamentality, fairness and inclusion, China has promoted five projects around the idea of "culture benefits the masses" that include an investment in a cultural information resources sharing project, radio and television coverage, a "farmer's bookstore" project, a rural film project and multi-use cultural centers in towns. Since the year of 2004,

Cultural Construction

On March 30th, 2007, the 15th China Content Broadcasting Network Fair was opened in Beijing. Exhibition area of the No.1 project of cultural construction of new countryside—"Radio and TV Village Through Village Project".

the free or preferential open system has been implemented in public cultural facilities such as state-owned museums, memorials, galleries, and conditional patriotism education base of all types and levels. The Chinese government decided to increase investment in cultural undertakings in the year of 2005. The national culture expense has totally reached 122 billion RMB with the average annual growth of 19.3% during the period of 11th five-year plan (2006-2010). In addition, the running and ensuring an adequate funding mechanism for public cultural institutions has been established based on the reasonable sharing of central and local systems of finance.

At present, public cultural service networks covering urban and rural areas have been preliminary created. By the end of 2013, the number of freely-opened museums and public libraries has reached 2780 and 3112. There are also 3298 and 34,139 cultural centers and multi-use cultural centers in towns around the country. Basically, multi-use cultural centers and farm house in villages have been built in almost every town and community. There are 221.2 square meters of mass cultural facility area for every 10,000 people. There are a total of 2579 radio and television broadcast agencies across the country. The number of television subscribers has reached 224 million. The number of digital cable television users has risen to 169 million. Radio shows reach 97.8% of the population and television reaches 98.4%.

Many cities have perfected their public cultural facilities at all levels forming the 15 minutes of public cultural services. Community cultural centers located in people's homes include libraries, electronic reading rooms, chess and card rooms and gyms, etc. Mass cultural activities are increasingly rich. The Shenzhen Municipal Government has held 14 reading month activities since 2000 to stir a passion for reading among the general public. In 2013, Shenzhen was honored with the title of "Global Model City of the Nationwide Reading Movement" by UNESCO.

The National Cultural Information Resources Sharing Project has basically built six levels of service networks since it launched in 2002. It has built a national center, 33 provincial branches, 2840 county centers, 28,595 service outlets and 602,000 administrative village grassroots service points. The construction of digital resources has topped 136.4 trillion bytes that have reached more than 1.3 billion people, the key embodiment of the gradual improvement of the construction of China's public digital culture. A project to promote the construction of a digital library has developed very fast. By the end of April 2013, the virtual network covered hundreds of libraries including the National Library since 2011. The promotion of the virtual backbone of the network is almost complete. Users at local libraries can not only access huge amounts of digital resources at the National Library but also benefit from the flow of data between provincial libraries that has been built to facilitate the sharing of digital resources and services.

Cultural Construction

The construction of the second phase of National Library of China is a key project in the tenth five-year plan of cultural construction. The newly-built library has been opened to public on September 9th, 2008.

China has worked hard to narrow the gaps in the construction of the public cultural service system. First, China emphasizes regional balance. Central and provincial financial departments have created special support funds to support cultural construction in older, minority, border or impoverished regions. During the 11th five-year plan (2006–2010), cultural construction in China's rural areas increased to 140.98% through the four years of the investment period. The investment in central and western region cultural construction increased to 133.8% and 154.5%. Nearly every township is equipped with a multi-use cultural center along with the basic achievement of Internet access ability while 100% of administrative villages and 95% of villages with more than 20-households are connected with telephone. The rural film project shows 8 million movies each year. It's basically feasible to show a film every month without charge in every village. The project is devoted to covering the country with digital cinema. The state invests more than RMB 18 billion to achieve uniform standards in more than 60 million rural bookstores, with 940 million

On February 20th, 2014, women of the Yao ethnic minority was reading in the farmer's bookstore of their village in Huangluo, Heping village, Longsheng Various Nationalities Autonomous County, Guangxi Province.

copies of books, 540 million audio and video products, 120 million electronic publications and sets of film projection equipment and reading materials.

In addition, the government operates extensive public cultural services for special groups and works to enhance the cultural rights and interests of teenagers, the elderly, rural migrant workers, the low-income and the disabled. The children's pavilion and digital library in the National Library officially opened in May 2010. More than 70,000 impaired people have benefit from the promotion of television programs by adding subtitles or sign language. Live and barrier-free online video services through the Internet have also contributed to the above mentioned results. In 2012, China's digital library for the blind and disabled provide millions of disabled people with barrier-free cultural services such as books, lectures and music. The construction plan of a public electronic reading room has been carried out at 28,612 villages, streets and communities to provide services oriented for teenagers, the elderly and rural migrant workers. The relevant state departments jointly issued *The Comments*

Cultural Construction

On May 31st, 2010, D-lib for children in the National Library was officially opened to the public.

on Further Strengthening the Cultural Work of Migrant Workers in 2011. Based on the public cultural services system, the paper aims to create a mechanism for cultural work among migrant workers characterized by the leadership of the government and the participation of enterprises and society.

Lastly, the 12th Five-Year Plan aims to protect the interests of minority cultures. By the end of 2013, there were 73 radio stations in national autonomous areas, 441 programs, 105 national language programs, 90 TV stations, 489 TV sets and 100 ethnic language programs. By the end of 2013, China had established 32 publishing houses for publishing ethnic books in 23 ethnic languages, 13 A/V pubishers in ethnic languages, 233 ethnic language periodicals, 99 ethnic language newspapers and 9429 books in ethnic languages. National autonomous areas have 50,834 cultural institutions of various kinds, including 653 libraries, 784 cultural centers and 385 museums.

The Ministry of Culture has actively carried out a series of national frontier line activities for cultural volunteers since 2010. In the past three

Contemporary China's Culture

On November 11th, the news center of the 18th National Congress of the Communist Party of China held a joint press conference, themed "cultural system reform and the construction of public culture service".

years, more than 50 supported groups have been built united by more than 20 municipalities and departments with more than 2000 cultural volunteers. They have organized more than 450 artistic performances in 12 frontier ethnic areas and the Xinjiang production and construction corps group and have held more than 2000 hours of business training. A series of cultural exhibitions over 600 days have benefited hundreds of people.

In 2013, the Central Budget invested 17 billion yuan in public cultural service system construction, up 1.6 billion yuan, or 10.55%, year on year. The funds were mainly used in grassroot, rural areas, old revolutionary bases, ethnic group areas, remote and poverty-stricken areas. The construction of a public cultural service system has resulted in practical benefits to the people at the grassroots level, and the government is making even greater efforts. At present, governments at all levels and state-owned cultural institutions are working together while enterprises and local public welfare units need to participate further. Funding and key cultural projects to benefit people are scattered across various departments as a result of a lack of coordination and integration. The comprehensive benefits have not yet taken full effect. A lack of resources and structural imbalance has led to a failure to satisfy the demands of the masses. The number of full-time public cultural teams is seriously insufficient. The rural culture administrator team is not stable enough and has uneven service levels. The difference between regional urban and rural development is still large. The Chinese government is working to perfect the system, improve efficiency and promote equality to realize the standardization, equalization and socialization of public cultural services. The first step is to deepen institutional and mechanism reforms and speed up the transformation of the government function to build the public cultural administrative system combining micro-management of cultural administrative departments with macro-management of industry. The structure of corporate governance should be promoted in public cultural institutions such as libraries, museums and cultural centers. The coordination mechanism for the public cultural service system should be accelerated to carry on overall planning and develop the reasonable configuration national public cultural resources, channels and carriers. The second step is to promote the central government budget by intensifying transfer payments to mid-western areas, poverty-stricken areas, ethnic minority areas and frontier regions according to the standards of basic public cultural services. The third is to guide and encourage social forces to participate in pubic cultural services to diversify supply subjects and methods in public cultural services. A performance-oriented evaluation mechanism should be established to perfect institutional guarantees for the efficient construction of public cultural services. The planning goal is the enrichment of cultural products and the basic construction of a public cultural service system by the year 2020.

Cultural Relic and Heritage Protection

China's long history and diversity have given modern China a rich cultural heritage. The protection of cultural heritage protection is regarded as a key aspect in the cultural construction of China so as to inherit Chinese civilization.

After the establishment of New China, the central people's government enacted decrees, established institutions, and forbid smuggling and destructive activities. That greatly changed the history of destruction and expropriation of cultural relics. The ministry of culture set up a cultural heritage administration. A cultural relics unit was built nationwide with archaeological institutes, museums, memorials and ancient architecture protection research institutes as

On December 16th, 2007, "Application for World Heritage for Beijing-Hangzhou Grand Canal" delegation of the CPPCC was making an on-the-spot investigation.

Cultural Construction

members. They were responsible for cultural genetic investigation, discoveries, research and protection as well as the cultural ethnic collections, custody, research and exhibitions. The state council enacted the *Provisional Regulations on the Protection and Control of Cultural Relics* and listed the first batch of 180 national key cultural relics' under protection in 1960. The State Council organized a national cultural relic census in 1981. And at the next year the government released the first batch of 24 famous historical and cultural cities and the second batch of 62 protected national key cultural relics. The *People's Republic of Cultural Relics* was formulated this year. Since the turn of the century, China has revised the *People's Republic of Cultural Relics*. The State Council has released successively the *Regulations for the Implementation of the Law on the Protection of Culture Relics* (2003), *Rules on Great Wall Protection* (2006) and *Regulations on Protecting Historical Famous Towns and Villages* (2008). For nearly 60 years, China has released more than 400 relevant laws, department regulations and normative documents involved heritage protection. China cultural heritage protection has embarked on a track of legalization and standardization. The second Saturday in June every year is set as Chinese Cultural Heritage Day in an effort to create an atmosphere of social attention, responsibility and shared achievements.

Cultural Relics Protection obeys the rules of "protection-oriented, first rescue, reasonable exploitation and further management". China completed the third national cultural relic census in 2011. The number of registered investigations of immovable cultural relic is nearly 770,000. The state council announced seven batches of national key cultural relic protection units for a total number of 4295, including 119 historical cities, 350 historical and cultural town villages. A multitude of new type cultural heritages rich in historical, artistic and scientific value has been fully emphasized such as industrial heritages, vernacular architectures, heritages in 20th century, cultural routes and landscapes. The Great Wall resources investigation fieldwork throughout the country has been completed to build the Great Wall of China resources

On February 23rd, 2010, contract signing ceremony of China-Kenya Archaeology Cooperation Program in Lamu Islands was held at Wangfujing Grand Hotel by National Museum of China, Department of Archaeology of Peking University, and Kenya National Museum.

information system. By the end of 2013, the amount of world heritage sites in China added to the *World Heritage List* reached 45, ranking the second in the world. The list in China contains 31 world cultural heritage sites, four world cultural and natural mixed heritage sites and 10 world natural heritage sites. The tasks of Silk Road International Joint Properties and Grand Canal Protection and Application are in full swing. China is actively involved in a series of tasks such as the International Cultural Heritage Protection Project, International Action in Cambodia's Angkor Monuments Restoration, Free Aid in Mongolia Bogurda Khan Palace Museum Maintenance and Archaeological Cooperation Research Project with Kenya.

China has collected 28.64 million pieces of cultural relics in the Chinese cultural relics system in 2292 museums and 551 industry museums. There

Cultural Construction

is still a large number of relics collected in other state-owned units and by people. There are 479 private Chinese museums. The museum is the platform of cultural relic exhibition whose free opening has been incorporated into public service system construction. In addition to basic exhibitions, there are more than 10,000 national museum exhibitions every year that attracted 637.77 million visitors in 2013 alone.

China used to be a nation lost in cultural treasures. From the Opium War in 1840, because of war booty, stealing, smuggling and illicit trade, a multitude of national treasures were lost all over the world. In 1997, China joined the *Stolen or Illegally Exported Cultural Convention*. China has signed bilateral agreements with 14 countries searching for lost or plundered cultural relics and has managed to retrieve over 3000 Chinese cultural relics lost overseas. China legally and successfully reclaimed 49 precious cultural relics stolen from the Hebei Chengde Summer Resort museum from an auction company in Hong Kong. The Tianjin Tanggu clock taken by the Eight Allied Armies as trophies was returned in 2005. China has set up National Engineering to repurchase

On April 26th, 2013, the French Pino family announced that they will make free donations of old Summer Palace's bronze rat and rabbit heads.

119

relics and invest funds to recover relics. More than 10,000 pieces of cultural relics has been solicited. The French Pinot family announced the donation of a bronze rat and rabbit head from the Summer Palace lost overseas.

China has carried out more than 26,000 cultural relic protection projects to strengthen the management of world cultural heritage sites, great historical and cultural cities or towns and cultural relic protection sites. Some 1272 endangered national key cultural relics have been basically excluded from the first to the fifth batches and over 3000 pieces of endangered cultural relics are in the sixth and seventh batch and moving forward. The Three Gorges project is a civil project. The archaeological excavations started first and lasted 10 years. Later, the project broke ground and moved forward to rescuing and protecting cultural relics. *Post-Wenchuan Earthquake Restoration and Reconstruction Regulations* include protection of Tibetan and Qiang cultural artifacts. The Maoxian county museum of Qiang people and the Beichuan Qiang Folk Museum are being built. The Ancient Building Group of Dujiangyan Post-

Lucun Village, Yixian County, Anhui Province is famous for exquisite wood carving buildings of large scale. It enjoys the reputation of first buildings in China, which is the essence of Hui-style architecture.

Cultural Construction

disaster Rescue Protection Engineering is completed. China continuously expands the cultural relic area through cultural relic protection projects such as the big cultural heritage ruins, contemporary and modern cultural relics, 20th Century industrial heritage and more.

Ancient Chinese architecture can also be protected through activation. The first step is to develop tourism based on the rules of "development in protection and protection in development". Funds from the government are guaranteed to facilitate repairs and attract visitors. The tourism income can be used to make up for the lack of protection funds. Another way is to reorganize and relocate cultural relics. Scattered old buildings have to be gathered in a new place to recreate original features.

With the acceleration of China's urbanization process, some of the ancient dwellings bearing thousands of years of Chinese history and memory have been abandoned or demolished such as Huizhou style buildings, Beijing courtyards and Shanxi courtyards, which are disappearing quickly. Some experts have proposed putting excellent vernacular architecture cultural heritage into significant components of urbanization strategy. And some local governments have realized the urgency and seriousness of this problem and formulated related policies to implement the rules of "archaeological survey prior to land plotting" avoiding damage to precious ancient buildings. More and more attention is paid to the unique cultural value of old buildings.

The protection of ancient Chinese books is also moving forward. Since March, 2008, the State Council has released the fourth *National Rare Ancient Books List* that contains 11,375 precious ancient books and 2000 national ancient book collections. The key projects of the National Project for the Recompilation of Qing Dynasty Historical and Chinese Ancient Books Collection and Protection Plan continues to be implemented. The key national publishing projects by the Ancient Chinese Book Digital Publishing and Chinese Dictionary Compilation Publishing are in progress. The relevant work is now focused on the rescue of ancient national cultural relics, the research and collection of minority ancient books such as the compilation of *Chinese Ancient Books Catalogue Abstract and Chinese Ancient Books Catalogue Abstract of Ethnic Minorities*. The government has done a lot for edition and publishing and translation to the classical old epic and excellent minority literature such as Gesar, Jiang Geer and Manas so as to bring the protection and research function of higher education schools and academic institutions into full play.

The Chinese Academy of Social Sciences History Organization has set up a Compilation Committee of the *Extraterritorial Chinese Rare Library* and published the Extraterritorial Chinese Rare Library which is the first cultural effort to systematically arrange ancient Chinese books on a large scale. Three series of *Extraterritorial Chinese Rare Library lists* have been released including more than 600 pieces of literature held overseas such as rare literature from the Song and Yuan Dynasties, precious engravings from the Ming and Qing Dynasties, old written drafts and classical literatures. Most of them were published in China first. There are estimates that more than 800 copies of archives including more than 2000 pieces of rare Chinese literatures taken out of country and embody the essence of 10 million Chinese literature that are held in more than 50 countries.

Intangible Cultural Heritage Protection

China's intangible cultural heritage protection started at the beginning of the 21st Century. Yunnan province first passed the *Yunnan National Traditional Folk Culture Protection Regulations* on October 17, 2013. UNESCO issued *Safeguarding of Intangible Cultural Heritage*. China joined the convention on preserving Cultural heritage in August 2004 to actively meet its treaty obligations and learn from other countries' protection experience as well as participate in international exchanges and cooperation. In 2005, the State Council promulgated the *Opinions of Strengthening Intangible Cultural Heritage Protection Work* and *Notice on Strengthening Culture Heritage Protection* to issue guidelines and suggestions for intangible cultural heritage

On December 11th, 2013, shadow puppet play in Yichang, Hubei Province. Shadow play has a history of more than 2000 years, but now this ancient and magical traditional art becomes a "shadow elf" out of sight.

protect task, which marks the spread of efforts to protect intangible cultural heritage. The State Council published the first State-level Intangible Cultural Heritage List in 2006. The ministry of culture evaluated and issued the first National Intangible Cultural Heritage Representative Inheritors Directory in 2007. The next year, 2008, the Ministry of Culture issued the *Identification and Management Measures of National Intangible Cultural Heritage Representative Inheritors*. *Intangible Cultural Heritage Law of People's Republic of China* was issued in 2011.

The first national nonmaterial cultural heritage census carried from 2005 to 2009 covered 870,000 pieces of investigation making the condition of national intangible cultural heritage clear including their origin, evolution, current situation, inheritor and protection measures of this project and its quantities. The protection plan was made on the basis of the above investigation. The 4-level (nation, province, city, county) directory protection system and national inheritor proclamation system were established as the fruits of the valid measures. The ministry of culture announced three lists with 1219 state-level intangible cultural heritage items and four lists that included 1986 national project representatives inheritors. The provincial intangible culture heritage lists published by People's government of various provinces (districts and city) include 9647 items. China has 31 kinds of cultural heritages included in the Human Intangible Cultural Heritage Representative List of UNESCO, such as Kunqu Opera, Guqin, Xinjiang Uygur Mukan, Mongolian tune folk songs, the Dragon Boat Festival, Chinese calligraphy, shadow play, and more. Seven items have been selected into the Intangible Cultural Heritage List in urgent need, bringing the total to 38. China has more items on the list than any other country in the world.

The Intangible Cultural Heritage Festival permanently settled in Chengdu in 2009 and is held every two years with the goal of demonstrating the intangible cultural heritage around the word and the country through exhibitions, performances and sales.

Cultural Construction

On June 15th, 2013, the 4th China Chengdu International Intangible Cultural Heritage Festival was opened in Chengdu. Through exhibiting, showing, and selling, it presented distinctive intangible cultural heritage from all round the world.

At present, intangible cultural heritage protection in China has entered into the overall protection stage characterized by integrity and a systematic effort to end one-off protection approaches. The main measures include the establishment of an intangible cultural heritage system, the distribution of intangible cultural heritage resources, the establishment of intangible cultural heritage inheritor pedigrees, the formulation to inheritor subsidies and the foundation of national folk cultural ecological reserves. Actions have been taken to protect endangered national cultural heritage of great value to the treatment of intangible cultural heritage such as the folk literature, culture, music, dance and ethnic epics.

For more than 10 years, China has established elementary intangible cultural heritage protection institutions keeping with China's national conditions and created work mechanisms of "government-dominated, society-participated, explicit responsibility and joint forces". The government-dominated methods are demonstrated in the aspects of legislation, planning, instruction and investment. The inheritors of intangible cultural heritage such as relevant institutions also play a fundamental role in protection, especially heritors that play a key role in the actual protection. According to statistics, the central government has invested RMB 2.10249 billion in the protection of intangible culture. In 2013, the funding for these efforts hit RMB 662.98 million.

Festivals and customs are essential contents of cultural heritage. The ethnic festivals and traditions receive special attention in Chinese society. A variety of folk culture activities in Han and minority festivals are held to demonstrate the content of festivals, customs and etiquette. The connotation of traditional folk festival culture is further explored by combining the inheritance with protection and the exploitation with utilization.

The abundance of intangible cultural heritage projects determines the diversity of protection methods. Ten kinds of intangible cultural heritage projects are applied the strategies of salvageable preservation, original eco-systems protection, productive protection and integrity protection. Starting from the principle of integrity protection, China has set up the national cultural ecological protection area to maintain cultural diversity and protect the integrity of the cultural ecological protection area as well as the richness of cultural resources. China has set up 15 state-level cultural ecological protection areas.

China has unfolded active efforts to protect endangered intangible cultural heritages. Since the 1980s, China has carried out the national folk integration project of literature and art to collect, arrange and publish traditional music, dances, dramas, folk arts, stories, myths, legends, ballads, proverbs, festival and long narrative poems. These include more than 400,000 folk stories, 500,000 proverbs, 200,000 ballads and 1,000,000 music materials digitized and preserved through audio, videos and pictures. The databases of opera, music, dance and fork art are in place. China has devoted much effort to the collection and management of national heroic epic poems. The Tibetan and Mongolian epic poems Gesar is the longest epic in the world relying mainly on the oral form to spread among people. There are more than 9000 recordings, some of which have been sorted.

China tends to inherit and develop precious folk cultural resource elements such as traditional Chinese craftsmanship, folk art, medicine pharmacy and diets by way of productive protection to adapt to the fluidity. The Ministry of Culture put out the first list of 41 demonstration bases of national intangible cultural heritage productive protection including Beijing cloisonné production techniques, Rongbaozhai woodblock watermark technique and mounts repair skills, Shanxi Laochencu brewing techniques, Jiangsu Yixing violet sand earthenware production technique, Tibetan Medicine and Uygur

From June 9th to 17th, 2010, "Wonderful workmanship Excelling Nature—Chinese Intangible Heritage 100 Arts and Crafts Masters Skill Exhibition" was held in Beijing Exhibition Center.

On August 15th, 2008, Living Show of Chinese Intangible Cultural Heritage Successors was held in Beijing Cultural Palace of Nationalities, which presented intangible cultural heritage of different nationalities in China. Wang Xisan from Hengshui was showing his inner painting skill.

musical instrument manufacturing. These folk cultures are maintained by the way of production to join modern social life. The productive protection method put forward by China has attracted global attention.

The protection of intangible cultural heritage inheritors is the key in the protection effort. As people grow older, the problem of lost intangible cultural heritage becomes more serious. Governments of all levels are working to improve and inherit the life and work condition of heritage subjects to create a favorable environment and attract young people to learn skills. The realization of replacement from the old to the young can ensure the smooth transmission of intangible cultural heritage.

China is such a vast area with many different customs. Some provinces and cities make the local regulations according to current conditions. Intangible cultural heritage protection regulations have been released in Xinjiang, Jiangsu, Yunnan, Zhejiang, Guizhou and Hubei. *Intangible Cultural Heritage Protection Regulations of Xinjiang Uygur Autonomous Region* was put out on April 4, 2008. Xinjiang is the hometown of song and dance and has three international intangible cultural heritage projects including Xinjiang Uygur Mukam, *Manas* and Meshrep[1]. China possesses 70 different national intangible cultural heritage lists and 237 items of autonomous region non-material cultural heritage projects. Cities and counties have established directories of their own with

On June 12th, 2012, master works of guqin, calligraphy, acupuncture, seal cutting, shadow puppet playing and other intangible cultural heritage were exhibited in National Museum of China. It is the exhibition of the version by Rongbaozhai woodblock printing.

Contemporary China's Culture

On March 19th, 2011, Khalkhas shepherds in splendid attire were performing *Manas*, the heroic epic to celebrate Nowruz Festival at People Square in Akqi County, Xinjiang Uygur Autonomous Region.

nearly 30,000 items covering 10 categories such as folk literature, traditional music and dance, operas and physical exercises. The proportion of minority sports events is 95% and the category items such as folk custom, traditional music, dance and skills are over 60%.

  China's 515 representative projects of 55 ethnic minorities are included in the national intangible cultural heritage protection list. Almost 524 persons are honored as national intangible cultural heritage representative inheritors. There are five Ecological Protection Areas of Minority Culture established successively and 18 items from minority group are included in the Human Intangible Cultural Heritage Representative List and Intangible Cultural Heritage List in urgent need of protection by the United Nations. Since the year of 2009, the cumulative central fiscal investment of RMB 510 million has gone towards minority ethnic village conservation and development projects. The 600 village pilot projects can be found in 28 provinces. Intangible heritage

Cultural Construction

Musical entertainment Meshrep was held at Mukam Heritage Center in Xinjiang Uygur Autonomous Region.

cultural relic protection has protected traditional cultural resources with rich national, regional and pluralistic character.

The information age makes cultural heritage protection easier. Digital construction of culture has been put forward in the current five year plan (2011–2015) and cultural reform and development have been outlined to promote comprehensive digitalization of cultural resources, production, transmission and consumption. China has launched the national survey of cultural relics and has, since 2001, been building a database management system. The national system of cultural relic museums has collected cultural relic data and 3.87 million pictures of cultural relics have been taken. The implementation of the virtual Imperial Palace, digital Dunhuang and national digital library have been underway for several years accumulating the digitalized productions of the talking *Riverside Scene at Qingming Festival* and digital Dunhuang[2]. People have witnessed 220th Mogao Caves copied using digital techniques with squares of 124 meters and 5333 original pictures at the ICCIE of Shenzhen in May 2013. The complete image was finished using picture processing and matching. Later, people may be able to appreciate all the cave paintings and sculptures from the Qin period (AD 366) using a 3D virtual environment so as to satisfy the need to view, appreciate and research. The digitalized protection of the cultural relic project in Lhasa has been launched to develop the management of archives for the Jokhang and Ramoche Temple.

The realization of digital cultural resources is a significant way to activate Chinese cultural treasures, realize effective transmission and protect the heritage of Chinese culture.

Explanation

1. Manas is the Kirgiz hero epics. It mainly narrates Kyrgyz people's courageous struggle to create a wonderful life regardless of hardship and eulogizes a great love story. Meshrep is a dance and recreational activity form of the Daolang people. It's a dance-oriented large entertaining activity with many active participants.

2. The digitalized "Riverside Scene at Qingming Festival" in Palace museum provides people an immersive experience with the sounds of peddling and storytelling.

Development of the Cultural Industry

To develop the cultural industry and ensure it helps economic and social development is the basis of the construction of a culturally powerful country. The cultural industry started the 21st Century quickly on the fast track.

Initial Framework of the Cultural Market System

Due to limits of time and recognition, the Chinese government tended to manage culture by means of the planned economy. There was confusion between the commercial cultural industry and the non-profit cultural industry, which resulted in low investment in government-led public cultural industrial projects and caused the commercial cultural industry to depend on the government for a long time. In the new century, Chinese cultural development ideas have become clearer. Confirming the market attributes and industry attributes of culture is key adjusting cultural development. In October 2000, the fifth plenary session of the 15th CPC Central Committee approved the tenth five-year project that puts forward a number of cultural tasks including efforts to perfect cultural industrial policy, strengthen the construction and management of the culture market and promote related cultural industries.

In 2003, a division between the commercial and non-profit cultural industries was created to promote a large number of state-owned cultural units into qualified market players. China has basically completed reforming state-owned institutions into commercial ones in areas such as publishing, film and TV production and broadcasting TV, traditional state-owned art troupes and the first batch of current political class newspaper publishers and other state-owned enterprises. Taking the publishing system as an example, 570 presses have turned into enterprises except for the People's Publishing House, braille press, Tibetology publishing house and ethnic publishing house. More than 1600 non-political newspaper, over 3000 distribution companies, more than 2100 literary and art troupes and thousands of film and TV companies were also turned into self-sustaining, self-developing, self-disciplined enterprises. The reform

Development of the Cultural Industry

Thirteen heavyweights of publishers and distributors of China Publishing Group including People's Publishing House, People's Literature Publishing House, the Commercial Press, Zhonghua Book Company, Xinhua Bookstore Head Office was named "Aircraft Carrier" in Chinese publishing.

of a large number of new market bodies turned into an important force in the development of the cultural industry. According to statistics, by the end of 2011, there were more than 10,000 state-owned cultural enterprises, about 40% of which emerged from the process of culture structural reform after 2003. In 2013, there were 19 enterprises that reformed after 2003 selected into Top 30 cultural enterprises, about 63.3% of the list and 23 state-owned enterprises, including the China Arts & Entertainment Group (CAEG), Shanghai Cultural and Broadcasting Acting (group) Co. Ltd, China Film Co. Ltd, China International Television Corporation, China Publishing Group company, 76.7% of the Top 30, had sale revenue of 204.7 billion yuan, accounting for more than 80% of the total which reflects that state-owned cultural industries are the main force in the development of China's cultural industry. In 2014, the sale revenues of the Top 30 hit 245.1billion, the net assets reaching 207.6 billion and net profit 31.6billion. The main operating income and net assets account for 80% of the Top 30, suggesting state-owned cultural enterprise' leading role in cultural industrial development, and their responsibilities in the industrial chain's weak links, regional key regions, cultural infrastructure construction a number of state-owned cultural enterprises.

Culture structural reform encourages social capital to move into the cultural industry, offering private enterprises valuable opportunities. In 2004, the Ministry of Culture issued the *Guidance and Support on Cultural Development for Non-public Sectors of the Economy*; in 2005, the *Stipulations on Non-public Capital Entering into the Cultural Industry* was issued by the State Council, clearly defining the detailed fields into which non-public capital could enter. Private cultural enterprises have developed fast. There are more and more private investors moving into publishing, films, TV serials, cartoon production and game production and 80% of the market of the film industry lies in private enterprises. In the last decade, most of the box office earning for films came out of private pictures. In 2013, the total box office of Huayi Brothers' Movies broke through the RMB 3 billion marks. There were three films from Huayi among the Top 5 of Chinese movies. In the entertainment field, there are 2773 folk troupes in China, including more than 20,000 private cast members.

By the end of April, 2013, there were 698,000 cultural units or related units, including 607,000 commercial units and 91,000 public units with societies and foundations included. There were over 10,000 private culture and art troupes,

Development of the Cultural Industry

On May 5th, 2014, the Global Mobile Internet Conference was held in Beijing, with the theme on "The Perfect World".

with over 5000 mixed ownership enterprise and private broadcasting, films or TV production enterprises. Private enterprises account for over 80% of the printing field and more than 70% in publishing. There are over 14,000 major cultural industries in Shanghai, including 12,000 non-public enterprises, which account for 88%. In the field of cultural entertainment, the online game industry and artistic works management, and non-public cultural enterprises account for over 95%. Nine private cultural enterprises were chosen into the top 30 cultural enterprises, i.e. , Beijing Wanda, Huangzhou Songcheng, Shengzhen Huaqiang and Enlight Media and others. only four private cultural enterprises were listed in Top 30 in 2009. All of China was initially created with public capital as the main body, with the diversification of private and foreign capital, while private cultural enterprises gradually become the important force in the promotion and development of the cultural industry.

The basic framework of China's cultural market system has been formed,

Contemporary China's Culture

On December 1st, 2009, Sohu New Perspective Economist Monthly Forum was held in Beijing. Experts and scholars attending had a serious discussion on "the state advances, the private sector retreats" and other subjects.

while all levels of activity are visible in the market. However, in contrast, the innovation of the systems and mechanisms are still inadequate, with too much intervention from the government allocating market resources. The initiative of enterprises in the market should be strengthened. The proportion of the state-owned economy is too high, and that of private business is too low. It is necessary to promote cultural diversification. The cultural market system is incomplete. Talent, information, logistics and infrastructure need further innovative systems and mechanisms. Improving the modern cultural market system and encouraging the development of the non-public cultural enterprises is also important. Lower the barriers to social capital so that capital and talent will be introduced into the cultural field. Help all kinds of factors of production flow faster and conclude the transaction to further arouse the vitality of the market.

Booming Development of the Cultural Industry

China's cultural industry mainly refers to industries that produce cultural products and provide cultural services, including traditional industries such as art, broadcasting, films and TV, news publishing, arts and crafts, cultural goods production and new industry industries such as cultural creativity, digital publishing, mobile multimedia, cartoon and game design, cultural recreation and more.

In the 1990s, Great Britain put forward the concept of a cultural creativity industry. The cultural industry was included in the tenth Five Year Plan, from 2001 to 2005. From then on, China issued a series of policies to guide the development of the cultural industry. In July 2009, the first special plan for the cultural industry was issued, *Revitalization Planning of Cultural Industry*. In the plan, the cultural industry was elevated as a strategic industry in China. In October 2010, the twelfth Five Year Plan, from 2011 to 2015, put forward the idea that promoting a cultural industry into a national pillar industry. In 2011, the sixth plenary session of the 17th CPC Central Committee approved the idea that to promote the cultural industry with a great-leap-forward in development to make it an important supporting point for the strategic economic restructuring, as an important point in the transformation of the pattern of economic development. According to international practice, the output of a pillar industry should account for over 5% of GDP. To implement the guidance in the sixth plenary session of the 17th CPC Central Committee and Cultural Reform and Development Outline in the twelfth five-year plan in February 2012, the Ministry of Culture put forward the *Cultural Industry Redoubled Plan*, confirming 11 key supported industries, including entertainment, amusement, cartoon, gaming, cultural traveling, works of art, art and craft, cultural exhibition, creative design, web culture and digital cultural service industry. The 11 key industries and their cultural products mostly have the characteristics of final demand orientation. In March 2014, the State Council issued Some Opinions on Driving the Integrated Development of Cultural Creation, Design Service and Related Industries to further integrate cultural creation and design service into seven major sectors like equipment manufacturing, consumables, building, information, tourism, agriculture and sports and the "greater circulation" of national economy.

Post of movie *Lost in Thailand*.

Development of the Cultural Industry

The movie *Finding Mr. Right* has a box-office of over 350 million RMB yuan

With the promotion of the cultural industry policy and Chinese historical and cultural resources, resource superiority is easily turned into industrial advantage and the cultural industry is developing fast, especially in the field of films, TV and publishing. In 2003, the output of Chinese films did not reach 100. In 2013, China produced 638 feature movies and 186 science and educational, documentary, cartoon and special movies. China became the third largest producer of films in the world. In 2002, the box office in China could not reach RMB1billion, while in 2010 it topped RMB10 billion and RMB20 billion in 2012 and by 2013 it hit RMB 21.769 billion, i.e. 24 times expansion within 11 years, with receipts from domestic films at RMB12.767 billion, accounting for 58.65%, with year-on-year growth of 54.32%. The box office of imported films reached RMB 9.002 billion, accounting for 41.35% of the total, falling 10% over the previous year. In 2013, there were seven films in the top 10 box office, such as *Thailand List*, *33 Days*, *Finding Mr. Right*, *So Young*

Contemporary China's Culture

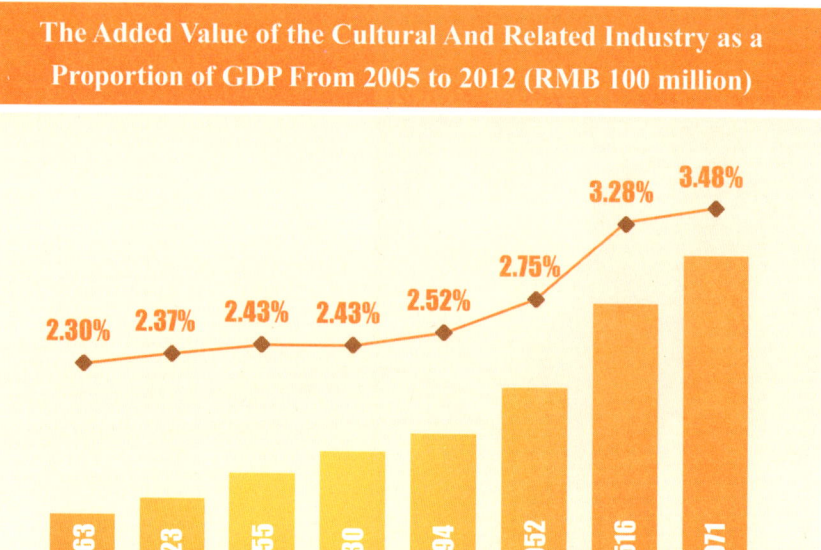

and *American Dream*. American media reports said China had made amazing progress in the film market this year. It said China had embarked on a journey of genre films, becoming one of the important competitors with Hollywood. Though the above view was exaggerated, the Chinese film industry has grown fast. There are 18,000 films in all. However, attendance in Chinese cinemas is only 15%, with some low-quality films. This is the reality of the Chinese film industry.

In 2013, China produced 441 TV series with 15,783 episodes, the most in many years. The output of television animation added up to 199,132 minutes. This year, newspaper output was 47.6 billion, periodicals added up to 3.4 billion and books 8.3 billion. China was the largest producer in terms of variety and volume. China was the second largest e-books producer in the world. China deserves to be known as the world publishing superpower. In 2012, the

Development of the Cultural Industry

added value of the publishing industry was 1663.53 billion, growth of 14.2% over a year earlier. Digital publishing reached RMB 193.55 billion, up 40.5%. In 2012, the value of animation was RMB 47 billion.

The overall size and strength of the Chinese cultural industry has risen. The proportion of the cultural industry is increasing. In 2004, the added value of cultural industry reached RMB 344 billion, 2.15% of GDP. In 2013, the added value of the cultural industry reached RMB 2.1 trillion, about 3.77% in GDP. The contribution of the cultural industry was 5.5% of GDP, with an average annual increase of 23%, higher than the average annual growth rate of GDP in the same period. Reform is the path to a stronger China, which is also true for the cultural field.

The cultural industry has grown fast in some districts. In 2012, the added value of the cultural industry in Beijing reached RMB 147.49 billion, accounting for 8.2% of GDP, first in China. The added value in Shanghai is RMB 124.7 billion, 6.2% of GDP. The added value in Guangdong is RMB 270.65 billion, accounting for 4.74% in GDP. The newly developing cultural industry grows fast in the area, such as digital publishing and with RMB 30 billion, one fifth of China's digital publishing; animation and web game with RMB 30 billion and one third of China. The added value in Jiangsu is RMB 233 billion, accounting for 4.3% of GDP, including RMB 104.14 billion from cultural production, with growth of 38% over last year. The added value in Hunan is RMB 80.44 billion, accounting for 3.63% of GDP. The added value in Hunan adds up to 8% of economic growth, with an average annual increase of 20%.

The Difficulties and Potential of the Cultural Industry Development

However, compared with the world cultural industry, China still has a long journey. The proportion of the cultural industry in the United States is 27% of GDP with Japan, the second largest cultural superpower, 20% and Britain 11%. The total volume of the cultural industry is not that big in China. The contribution of the cultural industry to GDP is still too low. There are still some problems in China's cultural industry: the scale and total volume is small, the degree of industrial concentration and intensification is low as well, the level of marketing is poor, preliminary goods are more than enough, content originality is weak, there is little innovation in product or technology or branding, and only a few of enterprises have key techniques or independent brands. How can the cultural industry grow sustainably? The report of the 18th CPC National Congress notes that it is essential to promote the integration of culture and technology, to develop a new cultural industry, to scale up the cultural industry, concentrate it, specialize it. It also put forward the requirement to perfect the corporate governance structure of commercial cultural units to make the culture market prosperous. Those requirements point out the direction for the development of the cultural industry in future.

Plan scientifically and build the system for the cultural pillar industry. There are many potential cultural industries in China, such as cultural fields in intelligent, high-tech, innovation, info media, art, city views, ocean culture and recreation. It is essential for China to establish a modern cultural market system, to fully realize the marketization of IP, talent and capital, to perfect cultural economic policies, encourage the combination of financial capital,

Development of the Cultural Industry

On March 18th, 2007, CCTV Animation co., LTD announced establishment at Diaoyutai State Guesthouse Hotel in Beijing.

social capital and cultural capital, to cultivate the large-scale cultural brand, set up an industrial chain, to make qualitative leaps of the cultural industry. It is also important, by means of the market, to help cultural enterprises develop without barriers from different districts, different industries, and different ownerships, to build a large scale, intensified, specialized cultural industry. In addition, it is vital to build a network of radio, film and television, to establish a national level modern media group on broadcasting and TV, to integrate nationwide resources so as to develop the cultural logistics industry, to build up an influential book cultural base of distribution, to build a core cultural industry.

China's cultural consumption has been increasing rapidly with great market potential. It is essential to support and guide the cultural industry, to increase the supply capacity of cultural products and services to meet demand for cultural consumption. In 2012, the Beijing GDP per person reached US$ 13,797, including RMB 1658 of cultural consumption per person, only 4% of family income. Therefore, cultural consumption has great potential. Since 2012, the information media industry has grown as the leading industry of cultural industrial system. The development and reform of China's new media has moved to the integration-based and mobile-oriented direction. Users of new media have increased and popularized with the help of the mobile Internet and the Web. The newly developing media is good at sustaining innovation, so it grows dynamically with the ever-growing level of socialization. The data shows that the scale of information consumption reached RMB 1720 billion in 2012, with year-on-year growth of 29%, with a drive on new output of RMB 930 billion in related industries. By the end of 2013, the number of Chinese netizens reached 618 million, including 500 million mobile net users. Internet penetration has reached 45.8%, increasing by 3.7% year on year. The access to the Internet stimulates the consumption for screen cultural products and other related information consumption, such as e-books, films, cartoon, music, TV series and game.

It is obvious that China's cultural industry has developed fast with great potential.

Giving High Priority to Developing Education

Education is the cornerstone of modern civilization. Prosperous education will bring us a flourishing Chinese culture. Since entering the new century, China has implemented a national strategy of giving priority to education focusing on such facets as improving educational conditions, further popularizing education and continuously developing education reform. We have made notable progress in improving fairness in education, which has made great contributions to economic and social development. Today, China has achieved the goal of higher education popularization and accomplished the change from a big country with a large population to a strong country with huge human resources.

Contemporary China's Culture

Building a Modern Education System

At the beginning of China's reform and opening-up, Comrade Deng Xiaoping proposed that education should be geared to the needs of modernization, of the world and of the future, and that education should be a strategic focus in the cause of China's socialism modernization. In 1985, the Communist Party of China issued the *Decisions on the Reform of the Education System*. In 1995, Jiang Zemin proposed that we should implement the strategy of rejuvenating the country through science and education. These two steps accelerated the development of education.

In the new century, the Chinese government put forward claims such as

China Science and Technology Museum is a directly affiliated institution of China Association for Science and Technology. It is a national complex science and technology museum.

Giving High Priority to Developing Education

"talented personnel are the primary resource" and "for a county to become strong, it must first strengthen education", thus it has been widely accepted that priority should be given to develop education. In order to promote the scientific development of the educational cause, comprehensively improve the quality of our people and strengthen the nation through human resource development, the Chinese government formulated in 2010 the *National Medium- and Long-Term Plan for Education Reform and Development (2010-2020)* and issued measures to ensure that economic and social development planning gives first priority to education, that government financial funds gives priority to education investment and that public resources give priority to meeting the needs of education and human resources.

Giving priority to education, investments by the state in education have increased greatly over the years. Government spending on education totaled

On December 23rd, 2010, students of Zouping Experimental Middle School in Shandong Province was learning assembling computer at their innovation practice base.

RMB 1.5 trillion, which accounted for 3.65% of GDP in 2010 compared to 2.9% in 2002. Spending has increased 3.2 times and at an average rate of about 20% per year. In 2012, government spending on education reached RMB 2,223,623 million, which accounts for 4.28% of GDP. The growth in 2013 was 3%, and rural and poverty-stricken areas enjoyed preference.

Deepening reforms of the education system. The country has strengthened the top-level designs of educational reforms and innovation by organizing and implementing major projects and pilot reforms and strengthening reforms of the system to train talent, examination and enrollment systems, the modern school system, the education management system, and so on.

In terms of education management, governments at all levels have a clear responsibility and authority in managing all types and all levels of educational institutes. Compulsory education is under the leadership of the State Council and is planned and implemented by the people's governments at the provincial level and managed by the people's government at the county level. Vocational education is under the leadership of the State Council and participation of all society, planned and managed by governments of different levels, mainly by local governments. Higher education is under two-level management of central and provincial governments, mainly by provincial governments.

China has gradually straightened out the relationship between governments and schools and built a mechanism where schools run and develop themselves independently and autonomously. The state encourages and guides social forces to participate in the running of schools. Thus, a new structure has been formed where private and public schools develop side by side, public schools playing the leading role.

Private schools have developed rapidly but independently of public schools and have made contributions in expanding educational resources, optimizing the educational structure and promoting educational reform. In 2012, the number of private schools (including educational institutes) of all levels and types in the country reached 139,900 with up to 39,110,100 students. Among them were 115,400 pre-schools, accounting for 69.2% of all pre-schools in the country. There were also 698 high schools, accounting for 29% of the total and 2856 secondary vocational schools, accounting for 21.7% of the total.

In terms of government spending, China has established a sound fiscal mechanism for public education, strengthened the government's responsibility in public education security and established institutes and mechanisms that ensure that the government takes full responsibility for compulsory education, government spending plays the leading role in noncompulsory education and educational funds are raised from multiple channels.

Through these constant adjustments and improvements, China has established the basic framework of a socialist education system with Chinese characteristics and built a modern education system.

Achieving Free and Compulsory Education in Both Urban and Rural Areas

In the last 10 years, China continued to make education a strategic priority. The government has not only further popularized education, but exempted millions of students from tuition and fees in the rural compulsory education phase. The educational ideal of the Chinese nation over thousands of years has been "learning to teach" and "no child left behind" and it has now become a reality.

For a long time, the financing of compulsory education was the

From the new semester of 2006, new mechanism to ensure funding for rural compulsory education came to effect in Enshi Tujia and Miao Nationalities Autonomous Prefecture, Hunan Province, exempting 480,000 students on the stage of compulsory education from tuition fees in 8 counties and cities.

Giving High Priority to Developing Education

responsibility of the local governments and local people. Since the end of the last century, the central government has gradually integrated compulsory education funds into the public finances. Pilot projects were started in 2001 to exempt the costs of tuition, textbooks and subsidize living expenses for students from poor rural families in the compulsory education stage. By 2007, this practice was extended to all rural students from poor families in the compulsory education stage. Early in 1985, Tibet took the first steps to implement the "Three Offers" - offering free meals, free boarding and free schooling for students in agricultural and pastoral areas in their compulsory education. In June 2006, the measure of "fully integrating compulsory education into government finance" was written into the revised *Compulsory Education Law*. Free and compulsory education was fully implemented in both urban and rural areas from September 2008. In urban areas, 28 million sets of tuition costs and fees were exempted. Over 100 million school-age students from primary school to junior high school did not have to pay any tuition or fees. By 2010, counties all over the country popularized the nine-year compulsory education, with 100% of population coverage and 160 million students benefited. This is a significant milestone in the development of education in China.

In 2012, the consolidation rate of the nine-year compulsory education plan reached 91.8%. China has a shorter history than advanced countries in implementing nine-year compulsory education but the good news is that average schooling years reached more than 9.5 for those over 15 years old, surpassing the world average. The secondary gross enrollment ratio reached 85%, which is in-line with the average of advanced countries. The average schooling years of the newly-increased labor force approached 12.4, surpassing the world average. Free education started in 2012 for rural secondary vocational schools.

Improving Fairness in Education

Since the beginning of the new century, the country has striven to promote fairness in the area of educational opportunities, the allocation of public education resources, the education system and regulations, and more.

The government has rapidly increased financial support for education in recent years and ensured a balanced allocation of education funds with a focus on compulsory education, vocational education and preschool education in rural, remote, poor and ethnic minority areas, on students from families with financial difficulties and on building a high-quality faculty. Increasing the rate of government financing in rural areas surpasses that of the whole nation of

In recent years, to make education more equitable and allocate education resources rationally Wuan Education Bureau in Hebei Province has invested 10 million RMB yuan to improve education conditions comprehensively.

Giving High Priority to Developing Education

which central and western provinces are growing fastest. The statistical bulletin of national education expenses showed that public fiscal budgets on ordinary primary schools increased by 23.42%. Of these, expenses in rural areas increased by 26.30% with Guizhou Province being the fastest at 47.35%. This year, central government spending on compulsory education security totaled RMB 246.5 billion in rural areas.

Teacher qualifications are keys to improving rural education. The Ministry of Education took rural teachers into consideration and implemented measures such as the "Free Education Policy for Pre-Teacher" and the "National Primary and Secondary School Teacher Training Program". And 2011 witnessed a record with 78.6% of primary school teachers having a college education or above and 62.8% of junior high school teachers having a bachelor degree or above in all rural areas. In 2012, the State Council issued the *Advice to strengthening the construction of rural teaching staff*, which regulated unified standards for urban and rural teacher, changed long-standing discrimination and injustice for rural teachers and raised their pay.

The country has implemented several projects, including a national program to ensure the safety of primary and secondary school buildings and plans to improve the education quality at weak schools in rural areas. Between 2010 and 2012, the central government has spent RMB29.7 billion to build or rebuild facilities such as dormitories and canteens in hundreds of thousands of schools. In 2013, the central government allocated RMB20 billion for renovating campus and canteens in rural areas. Fundamental changes have taken place in the condition of primary and secondary schools in largely rural border areas.

China has set up a funded system to aid poor students, which benefits all students of all ages from pre-school to graduates. The government provides about RMB 100 billion each year, funding nearly 80 million students. By 2012, a little over 13 million resident students from poor rural families received a

Contemporary China's Culture

China stated the Nutrition Improvement Plan for Countryside Students, according to which every student get 3-yuan subsidy for lunch. Students were having lunch in Yuanan Central Primary School, Hubei Province.

living allowance. The government implemented a plan to improve the nutrition of rural students in the compulsory education stage. By 2013, totally 32.45 million rural students enjoyed nutrition aid subsidies during their compulsory education periods.

The government has initially ensured that the children of rural migrant workers have access to free compulsory education in urban areas. Now 1,393,870,000 rural migrant workers' children all over the country have had access to free compulsory education, which accounts for 9.7% of the total number of compulsory education students and of which 80.2% are in public schools. At present, plans for children of migrant workers to participate in the university entrance exam are moving faster than expected. In 2013, 30 provinces had announced the college entrance exam program for the children of migrant workers, and 12 provinces started to solve the problem.

Giving High Priority to Developing Education

In terms of special education, there were a total of 1853 special schools in 2013 with 43,700 full-time teachers and 378,800 students receiving special education. Of them, 65,700 students were enrolled into special schools that year. And 35,000 students learned in regular classes in primary and secondary schools, which have 199,800 students.

Using information methods to expand high-quality education resources, China is trying to build an effective mechanism and takes it as a means to gradually narrow gaps in different areas, the imbalance between the development of education in urban and rural areas as well as different schools. "Online classes" are increasingly common way of teaching in recent years. Relying mainly on wideband networks and video conferencing technology, excellent teachers from city schools and central schools lecture on music, fine

On July 16th, 2013, enrollment of children of migrant workers at Longgang Primary School in Hefei, Anhui Province. The school provided one-to-one service to the parents.

art and more in real-time to small rural schools. These excellent teachers also tutor students online with teachers from small rural schools. Through things like "online classes", children living in rural areas have access to quality education resources.

Obvious progress can be seen in China's education fairness, but there is still an imbalance in the development of education of various types and at different levels and imbalance education rights of disadvantaged groups and special groups. In some places, too many funds were used to help with the living costs of poor rural students, which far exceed spending on education itself. This is a function of poverty alleviation funds not education funds. Education funds should guarantee high-quality education, while poverty alleviation is a problem for civil authorities.

Rapid Development of Vocational Education

Since China's reform and opening-up, the government has issued a policy for developing vocational education in order to develop vocational talents to meet the needs of social and economic development. Skill-oriented talents, knowledge-oriented talents and multi-skilled talents are in great need for economic and social development, which led the government to support special education and make it a strategic priority along the same level as rural basic education and the construction of high-level university. In Oct. 2005, the State Council released the *Decision to Vigorously Develop Vocational Education* and

On November 11th, 2011, establishment meeting of Vocational Education Group of Loudi, Hunan was held at Loudi Vocational and technical college.

proposed reforming vocational education reform and development as part of the Eleventh Five-Year Plan (2006–2010).

In the Eleventh Five-Year Plan period, the government spent RMB 10 billion, to support the construction of more than 2300 vocational education training bases, more than 2680 county vocational centers and demonstration vocational secondary schools, 100 national demonstration higher vocation schools and organizational training for 150,000 professional teachers. China has set up a wide range of funding systems to help poor students in vocational schools, benefiting 90% of secondary vocational students and 20% of vocational college students.

To meet social demand for skilled talents, vocational schools have explored flexible and diverse models such as running schools with enterprises and enterprise groups and dialogue with industries. They have set up more than 50 kinds of featured professional educational paths with characteristics of national culture and folk arts and crafts. Vocational schools have developed a large number of talents and bases to inherit and spread intangible cultural heritage and play an important role in developing traditional culture and unique folk art.

In the last 10 years, China has made rapid progress in vocational education and has established the world's largest vocational education system. In 2011, there were 30 million students in secondary and higher vocational schools all over the country, about half of the number of junior high school and college students, respectively 48.89% and 47.67%. From 2002 to 2013, Chinese vocational schools developed more than 80 million skilled talents, who later became the main force in real economic industries. They also trained 185 million rural laborers. Vocational education contributes around 21% of the schooling years for laborers and has made great contribution to promote economic development and social progress, social justice and spreading national culture.

Giving High Priority to Developing Education

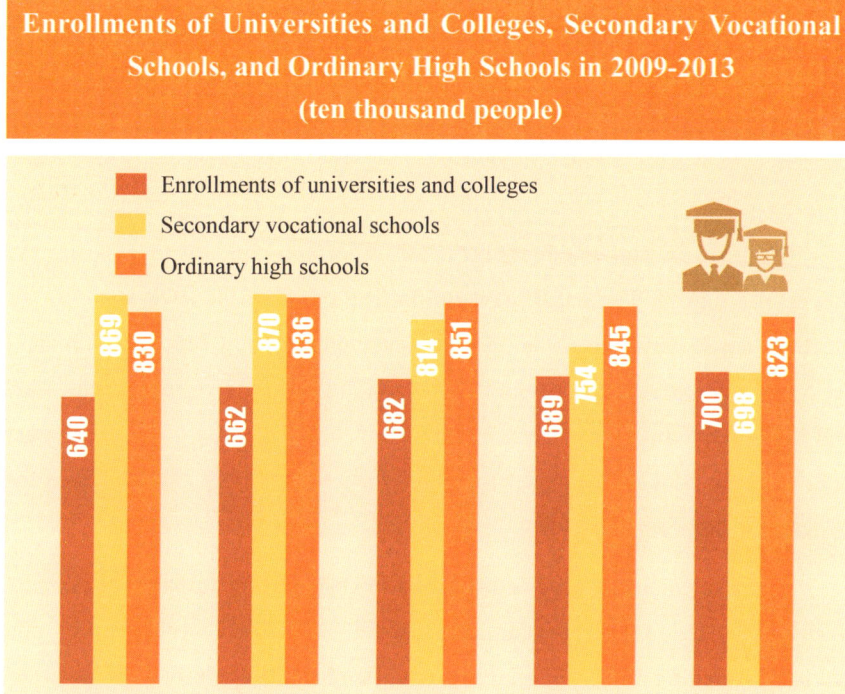

Data Source: *2013 National Economy and Social Development Statistics Bulletin.*

However, vocational education in China is more focused on expanding. There are problems in vocational schools, including the fact that the education is often too close to the requirements of enterprises and industries, teaching methods can not completely conform to social practice and the quality of talent training is generally low. Modern vocational education must adapt to the development of modern industrialization. A flexible education system should be built to develop new skills and employability, provide effective services for developing and redeveloping the skills of the labor force, make effective matches between supply and demand of skilled labor and cultivate high-quality workers to deepen cooperation with corporations.

Popularization of Higher Education

The level of higher education is an important standard to measure the power of a nation. The enrollment proportion of China in 1978 was 5%. To meet the needs of economic and social development, the Chinese government set out to popularize education in the Promotion Plan of 21st Century Education and expanded admissions to higher education. By 2002, the gross enrollment rate of higher education increased to 15% from 9% in 1999. That realized the popularization of higher education.

Universities and colleges continued to expand while emphasizing quality during the Eleventh Five-Year Plan period. In 2003, 22 universities and colleges including Peking University and Tsinghua University were awarded rights of self-enrollment. The central government continued to allocate funds to help implement the "211 Project" and the "985 Project" and started the "Plan for Building the International Demonstration Vocational Colleges" in 2006. The government implemented in 2007 the "Project of Teaching Quality and Teaching Reform in Colleges", which effectively pushed forward the reform of undergraduate education and teaching and promoted the quality of talent training.

In recent years, China's higher education entered into a stage of intensive development to maintain and improve teaching quality. The Ministry of Education issued the *Opinions on Comprehensively Improving the Quality of Higher Education*, putting forward overall requirements to stabilize scale, optimize structures, intensify advantages and emphasize innovation. The Ministry of Education and Ministry of Finance jointly launched the "211 Project" to put forward systems and mechanism reforms of universities

Giving High Priority to Developing Education

and colleges, taking national requirements and global reputation as the fundamental starting point and focusing on improving innovation capability with a combination of talent training, causes and scientific research. Guided by the Talent Development Plan, colleges and universities introduced 1171 innovation talents, accounting for 64% of the national total. Andrew Chi-Chih Yao (1946.12), a Chinese-American, won the A.M. Turing Award, the Nobel Prize of computing in 2000. As one of the top international scientists, he gave up his tenured faculty position in Princeton University and opened a computer science experimental class in Tsinghua University in order to develop world-class programmers.

The Ministry of Education and the Ministry of Finance have also issued the *Prosperity Plan for Philosophy and Social Science in Colleges (2011–2020)*. The goal of this plan is to improve colleges' ability to develop talents for

On April 23rd, 2011, Tsinghua University's 100th anniversary party was held in Beijing.

scientific research, social services and cultural preservation and innovation, comprehensively improve the quality of higher education and promote the development of the innovation system of philosophy and social science.

By 2012, there were 2790 universities and adult colleges (1018 in 2000) and 811 graduate institutions, of which 534 are universities and colleges and 277 are research institutes. The gross enrollment of higher education reached 30%, with a total of 33,252,100 students, which is the highest in the world.

To meet the demands of economic and social development, China optimized and adjusted the syllabus and structure of specialties and strengthened efforts to develop talents in such key fields as software engineering, integrated circuits, hydrologic and geological engineering, nuclear industry, information security and animation. All of these talents have played

On June 23rd, 2014, working meeting of national vocational education was held in the Great Hall of the People.

Giving High Priority to Developing Education

On June 11th, 2012, seminar of *"2012 Employment Blue Book Release and Cultivation Quality of Colleges and Universities"* was held by Chinese Academy of Social Sciences, during which the *2012 Employment Report of Chinese College Students* was released.

an important role in major national projects such as the manned space project, high-performance computer development, the Three Gorges Project, the construction of Qinghai-Tibet Railway and the Chang'e Project.

According to the data of the Sixth Population Census in 2010, 119 million people had higher education. In 2000, 3611 people per 100,000 had higher education and the number grew to 8930 in 2010. The number of employees with a higher education is among the highest in the world. The latest data has showed that in 35 years of postgraduate education, China has developed 4.2 million masters and more than 500,000 doctoral talents, almost 5 million highly educated people. These talents became the backbone of all walks of life and contributed to the development of various social undertakings. Education has significantly enhanced its ability to serve economic and social development. In

2010, among the National Award for Natural Sciences, Technical Innovation Award and Science Progress Award, 70% of these awards are won by talents in universities and colleges.

Further education in universities and colleges gives a chance for people to pursue lifelong learning. Presently, more than 1600 colleges among a total of 2000 offer part-time education and have developed more than 40 million talents from 2011 to 2012. By 2012, the number of registrations for various training courses in further education colleges rose to more than 50 million. Further education covers three aspects of education including academic education, career-focused training and community-oriented education in society, life and culture. The task for the future is answering questions of how to absorb further education into the teaching quality management and evaluation system, a well-run school-running system, integrate and develop good resources, strengthen corporation with enterprises in various fields, open course resources through digital technology and also further promote all the people to pursue life-long learning.

One problem in the development of colleges and universities is the relationship between universities and the government, who should work together to push forward in the building of a modern school system and change evaluation systems from executive-led evaluation to professional-dominated evaluation. Universities and colleges should have a clear ideal of how to run schools and sound values, prevent the atmosphere of fickleness and quick success and develop professional talents who are ambitious and can have a foothold in future society. According to the ranking of world universities by *The Times Higher Education* for 2012–2013, only four universities in China were among the top 100, 29 were from Europe. The quality and innovation of university education in China still needs to be improved.

Achieving a Leap-Forward Development of Ethnic Group Education

Many ethnic groups in China lived in the equivalent of slavery societies before entering modern society. Education in ethnic minority regions was lagging behind in 1949 when the People's Republic of China was founded. The Common Program of the Chinese People's Political Consultative Conference stipulates that the People's Government shall assist people of all ethnic groups to develop their political, economic, cultural and educational construction work. The state provides support for the development of ethnic minority education through funds and teachers. Universities and colleges of all kinds give preference to minority students. Languages of ethnic groups concerned or commonly used locally are used in teaching minority people. Backed by the state, ethnic minority education arose from nothing and a modern education system was established.

Since the reform and opening-up in 80's, the state issued guidelines every couple of years to implement the policy of ethnic minority education. In July 2002, the State Council released the *Decision on Deepening the Reform and Accelerating the Development Education Among the Ethnic Groups* and clarified the goal of "leaping-development of ethnic minority education".

The goal emphasizes that the government should give more support to education in remote pastoral areas, alpine areas, border areas and poverty-stricken areas inhabited by ethnic groups. During the period of the "Eleventh Five-Year Plan", the central government allocated RMB 5 billion in special funds for education in 12 western provinces and autonomous regions inhabited by ethnic groups. In 2007, the *Outline of the Eleventh Five-Year Plan for National Education* clearly stipulated that public educational resources would

On December 12th, 2011, schoolgirls of the Yao nationality were taking computer class at Shangsi Ethnic Middle School in the Guangxi Zhuang Autonomous Region.

be tilted in favor of ethnic minority regions, which where first to achieve the plan of nine-year free and compulsory education.

In the "Eleventh Five-Year Plan" period (2006–2010), the central government allocated RMB 27,818 million to guarantee education in five autonomous regions. Of the money, RMB 3030 million went to fellowships for secondary-level vocational students, RMB 1018 million went to tuition for secondary vocational students, RMB 350 million went to for national grants for high school students and RMB 6125 million for college scholarships. All of these guarantee the increase of educated populations in ethnic groups.

In order to accelerate the development of education in ethnic minority regions, the state implemented a mechanism to encourage ethnic groups in great need. Some of the universities, secondary vocational schools and adult universities opened a fair amount of college-prep classes for minority students.

Giving High Priority to Developing Education

The government made greater efforts to provide teacher training and encourage more in-service teachers to attend inland training and offered preferential policies to encourage graduates from colleges and universities to teach at community and village schools in ethnic minority areas. In 2006, the central government allocated special funds to recruit college graduates to teach in western rural schools. In two years, 33,000 teachers were recruited in special positions to teach in 4074 primary schools and schools in ethnic areas in 13 provinces and 395 counties in western areas.

The Chinese government has committed to develop "bilingual" teaching (teaching in a minority language and in Han Chinese) in areas inhabited by the ethnic groups and good results have been attained. According to rough statistics, there are more than 10,000 schools using 29 scripts of 21 ethnic groups to carry out bilingual teaching and the total number of students attending these schools is over 5 million. These ethnic groups include Mongolian, Tibetan, Uyghur, Kazak, Kyrgyz, Xibo, Korean, Miao, Bouyei, Dong, Hani, Bai, Yi, Naxi, Jingpo, Lihsu, Lahu, Va, Dai, Uzbek and so on.

Data from the Sixth Population Census in 2010 showed that the minority population was 113.79 million, accounting for 8.49% of the population. By the end of 2012, the number of minority students attending schools of all levels and all types in the whole country added up to 23,844,800, or 9.27% of the total. The number of minority students attending compulsory education was 15,154,600, of which 9.39% were in secondary schools and 10.7% in primary schools, more than the national average.

The years of schooling of 14 groups like Korean, Manchu, Mongolian and Kazak were above the national level. In 2011, the number of minority students attending universities and colleges reached 2.37 million, accounting for 6.67%, up by 338.08% from 2002. The gross enrollment of universities and colleges in minority regions has increased steadily and high school education has entered into the stage of popularization. Some 55 minority regions have their own

Contemporary China's Culture

On September 14th, 2012, students of the Hezhe nationality were learning to sing Yimakan storytelling, which is inheritance and protection of the Hezhe traditional culture.

college students. The number of college students per 10,000 in Uygur, Hui, Korean and Naxi surpassed the average level of the entire country. In order to adapt to economic and social development, colleges and universities in minority regions have strengthened the construction of applied disciplines and characteristic courses. For all, the overall cultural quality of minority peoples has achieved significant improvement.

Improvement of International Communication and Cooperation in Education

In 1978, in order to develop world-class scientists, Comrade Deng Xiaoping actively advocated sending more students abroad and emphasized that we should send as many as possible. In December 26 of that year, the first 50 students left Beijing for the US, with a stop in Paris, beginning the ice-breaking journey. Then appeared the largest and longest-lasting trend of studying abroad in Chinese history.

The Chinese government has helped citizens study abroad at their own expense. In 2002, the number of students going abroad totaled 125,000, among which 117,000 are self-funded students. After 10-year-plus development, the number of students going abroad increased to 413,900 in 2013, among which, 384,300 are self-funded students. Both of these numbers were 3.3 times of that in 2002.

In the process of China's higher education internationalization, the biggest problem is a brain drain. Of 3,058,600 students going abroad from 1978 to 2013 in the whole nation, 1,444,800 students returned to China. In the US, 22% of foreign scientists and engineers with Ph.D degree are from the Chinese Mainland. With the rapid development of China's society and economy, more and more students chose to return to China to work or set up their own businesses. In 2013, about 353,500 students returned home for development.

The number of foreigners studying in China has also increased. By 2008, China had set up relationships on cooperation and exchanges with 188 countries and regions. In 2013, China entertained 356,499 international students from 200 countries and regions, who studied in 746 universities, research institutes and other educational institutes from 31 provinces, autonomous regions and municipalities in China. The number of foreign students was 4.1 times that of 2002 (8,6000 international students then). Among these students, 25,687 received Chinese government scholarships and 266,924 are self-funded students. Compared to 2002, the number of countries providing overseas students increased by 49 and 351 more universities and colleges hosted overseas students. Students from Europe, America, Southeast Asia and the Middle East increased significantly, with 47,271 from Europe, accounting for 16.15% of total and 32,333 from Americas, accounting for 11.05% in 2011. Data suggested that students from the Americas increased by 18.75% from a year earlier. According to incomplete statistics, more than 10,000 students from Arab countries studied in China in 2012, up 70% from 2010.

Education itinerant exhibition of overseas universities held in Beijing.

Giving High Priority to Developing Education

Students would once come to China for short-term exchanges but there are now more and more foreign students that come to China to earn degrees. In 2013, 147,890 foreign students got degrees, making up 41.48% of the total, increasing 10.77% year on year. The number of international students enjoying Chinese governmental scholarship increased 4554, up 15.83% year on year. Mulatu Teshome, President of Ethiopia, was one student that came to China with funding from his government in 1976. He studied at Peking University and received his bachelor's degree, masters and Ph.D.

On October 20th, 2012, French exhibition stand in Chinese International Educational Expo.

The number of foreign students coming to China is growing and more and more "foreign faces" can be seen in universities and research institutes in full-time academic research. In 2012, China appointed 35,727 foreign experts and researchers, the largest number in China's education history.

Peking University has always been a bridge to promote mutual exchanges and learning between eastern and western cultures since its foundation and now employs qualified and experiences teachers and the best students from all over the world. In 2012, for example, Peking University had more than 1000 foreign experts and teachers, more than 2400 international students in reading and more than 6000 international students coming to study or visit China. And more than 2000 international expert seminars were held.

China's universities encourage students to study abroad for about a year, including exchange programs, overseas internships, international conferences and entertainment communications. Some prestigious universities made great efforts to promote students to study and intern abroad so as to improve the employment competence of graduate students and to broaden channels of international exchanges.

The number of Chinese-foreign cooperatively-run schools is growing. For now, quite a number of higher education institutes of these kinds have been established such as Xi'an Jiaotong-Liverpool University co-founded by the University of Liverpool and Xi'an Jiaotong University, NYU Shanghai by East China Normal University and New York University and the University of Nottingham Ningbo China co-founded by Nongbo University and the University of Nottingham. What's more, Chinese-foreign cooperative projects were organized in hundreds of colleges and universities and dozens of specialties and promoted the cultivation of highly qualified international talents.

China's education has contributed to cultivate hundreds of millions of high-quality laborers, professionals and top innovative talents. The

Giving High Priority to Developing Education

On October 15th, 2012, establishment ceremony of New York University Shanghai was held in Pudong, Shanghai. The university was co-established by China and the US.

development of education has greatly improved the quality of the people and put forward scientific innovation and cultural prosperity. It has also made great contributions to economic development, social progress and the improvement of people's well-being. In China, the goal that all children can "receive an education" has been guaranteed, but the current education situation still falls considerably short of what people expect. Problems need to be solved in China particularly around how to allocate high-quality education resources, how to realize education fairness, how to improve the overall quality of teachers, how to reform the management and evaluation mechanism, how to change the current atmosphere of fickleness and quick success, and, most importantly, how to guarantee that every child receives a good education.

Development and Innovation of Science and Technology, Philosophy and Social Sciences

Under the guidance of the strategy of rejuvenating the country through science and education, Chinese science and technology have achieved great development and progress, while the basic research of natural science and high and new technology have also achieved fruitful results and China has taken a leading position in the aspects of space exploration, super computers and high speed railway. China has gradually been entering the international innovation network and has acquired, innovated and shared knowledge on the frontier of science and technology. The philosophy of the social sciences that plays a guiding role in social development has received unprecedented attention. China is now paying attention to the establishment of a unique innovation system.

Enhancement of National Technology Innovation

When establishing the scientific research system, the new China attached importance to the independent development of science and technology and promoted the innovation of science and technology. After the reform and opening-up policy, Deng Xiaoping suggested that "science and technology are the primary productive forces", which has had deep influence on the development of science and technology.

In the early 1980s, China had launched several recoverable remote-sensing satellites. In 1983, using homemade materials, China designed and researched the first giant computer named "Galaxy" with a computing speed

On May 18th, 2012, exhibition of model of Beijing Electron Positron Collider.

100 million times per second and the first "757" computer with computing speed of 540,000 times per second. The "863" Projects carried out in 1986 promoted the establishment of the Beijing Electron Positron Collider and other main scientific engineering projects. The Qinshan Nuclear Power Plant linked to the grid and the world-class Galaxy giant computer was born. China achieved great development in many important scientific and technological fields such as space technology, high-energy physics, biology, medicine and health, geoscience and chemistry.

In 1995, the CPC (Communist Party of China) Central Committee and the State Council proposed a strategy of rejuvenating the country through science and education and elevate science and technology to the national strategic level and carried out the deployment. Basic research is the source of independent innovation. In 1997, China proposed a key basic research and development program ("973" Program) that took key national demands as its orientation and mainly supported basic research, which faced key national strategic demands, such as agriculture, energy, information, resources and environment, health, material science, manufacturing and engineering, comprehensive interdisciplinary science and key scientific frontiers.

The new round of the scientific and technical revolution developed rapidly and international economic, scientific and technological competition became more fierce in the 21st Century. In 1999, China proposed the idea of establishing the national innovation system. In 2006, China publicized the medium and long-term science and technology development plan and formally put forward the decision of enhancing independent innovation ability. The government established the collaborative innovation system with its main part of enterprises and the combination of industrial, national and college science and technology. Also it developed a series of policies and measures in finance and taxation, government procurement, intellectual property rights protection and talent construction, in order to facilitate innovation.

Contemporary China's Culture

On November 7th, 2013, Huawei's exhibition stand at Shanghai Industry Fair.

In March 2009, China introduced documents underlining the support and promotion of the stable development of the economy, launched 12 key scientific and technological projects such as large-scaled integrated circuit and software, information safety and electronic government affairs, electronic finance and the electric automobile and improved the core competitiveness of key industries. In 2010, the government paid attention to the cultivation and development of seven strategic new industries, such as energy conservation and environmental protection, new-generation information technology, biology, high-end equipment manufacturing and new energy. In early 2012, the No. 1 Document of the CPC Central Committee was themed "Accelerating the Agricultural Science and Technology Innovation", which highlighted the development of agricultural science and technology.

In order to realize innovative development, China increased investment in scientific research (rather than investments in infrastructure and mechanical devices) on one hand and improved the educational level on the other. With the rapid growth of GDP, investment in scientific research in China increased continually. In 2006, investment in scientific research was RMB 300 billion and it increased to RMB 861 billion in 2011. As a percentage of GDP, spending increased from 1.42% to 1.83%, a growth rate of over 20% per year. In 2013, expenditure in R&D was RMB11.906 trillion, up by 15.6%. The spending accounted for 2.09% of GDP and ranked second in the world (investment in scientific research in Europe accounted for 2.2% GDP).

The development of education and the support of the government for research resulted in a large number of talents over 30 years. In 2010, the total

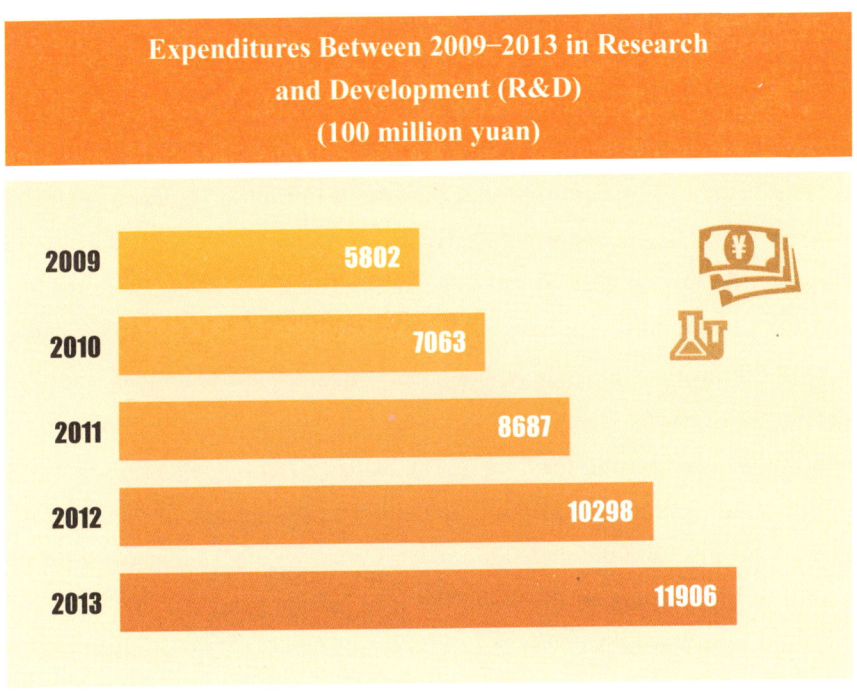

Data Source: 2013 National Economy and Social Development Statistics Bulletin.In 2013, the R&D expenditure was RMB1.1906 trillion, up by 15.6% and equivalent to 2.09% of gross domestic product (GDP).

number of human resources in science and technology reached 57 million in China. It was first in the world, an average annual increase of 8.6% over 10 years. In 2013, the total number of research personnel hit 3.2 million. Total 130 state engineering research centers were built and there were 128 state engineering labs. There were 149 state-district joint engineering research centers and 180 state-district joint engineering labs. There were 887 enterprise technology centers certified by the state and the number of provincial-level enterprise technology centers reached 8137. The total R&D expenditure of enterprises in Jiangsu, Shanghai and Tianjin exceeded the total number of Italy and Spain. The investment in research of Lenovo Group in 2013 topped $ 500 million. In 2012, the total value of output of high technology industries broke the record of RMB 10 trillion, while the total number of high-tech zones was 105 with gross revenue of RMB 16.1 trillion.

The increase in research investment had a visible effect. The number of international publications of China was the second in the world and China obtained a series of major original achievements in neutrino research, quantum communications and super-conductivity. The number of patents in China surpassed the U.S. in 2011. In 2013, the number of patent applications at home and abroad continued to grow and hit 2.377 million, up 418,000. There were 2.21 million patents at home, about 93%. China accepted 825,000 invention patent applications from home and abroad, including 693,000 domestic applications, accounting for 84.0%. The annual patents granted reach 1.313 million cases, including 1.210 million domestic applications, or 92.2% of the total. Altogether 208,000 invention patents were granted, including 138,000 domestic applications, or 66.6% of the total. In the year, 295,000 technical contracts were signed in China and the volume of transactions was RMB746.9 billion, up by 16%. In 2013, Chinese enterprises acquired 79,000 invention patents, which accounted for 54.9% of the total domestic total number. The status of innovative subjects of enterprise intellectual property was increasingly consolidated. Huawei Technologies and ZTE were ranked among the five enterprises with the most international patent applications in the world. In general, the innovation and R&D expenditures of China's large and medium-size enterprises only account for 1% of its operating revenue, much lower than that (5%) in developed countries. And the conversion of sci-tech achievements to technical applications is much lower than that in developed countries. Many scientific achievements have not been converted into applicable technologies.

Contemporary China's Culture

New Breakthrough of Science and Technology

More and more Chinese now show up among the most important breakthroughs of science and technology. In terms of nanotechnology standardization, China has kept step with the world and participated actively and partly guided the international nanotechnology standardization. As for the research fields of space remote sensing, information safety, marine equipment and carbon fiber material, China also made a series of breakthroughs.

In October 2000, the first "Beidou Navigation Test Satellite" developed by China was launched successfully. In 2012, "Beidou-2" finished regional networking and started providing satellite navigation, covering most of Asia-Pacific.

Model of Beidou navigation test satellite in Nanjing Science and Technology Museum in Jiangsu Province.

On October 24, 2007, the first lunar probe "Chang'e-1" developed independently by China was launched from the Xichang Satellite Launch Center deep inside the Daliang Mountains. There was only one mid-course correction and then it completed a hard landing, which realized the Chinese dream of a moon landing. At 15:05 in November 12, 2008, the first full map of the moon's surface filmed by Chang'e-1 was published, which is the most complete map published in the world. In October, 2010, it took just 112 hours for Chang'e-2 to fly to the moon. On December 14, 2013, Chang'e-3 with a craft carrying the "Yutu" lunar rover landed on the moon and completed a soft landing in the Sinus Iridium District. This was the first human detector that returned to the land of the moon since 1976. "Yutu", the unmanned detector stayed on the moon for about 90 days. Other than investigating the geology of the moon's surface, it also explored the soil 100 meters under the ground by radar. China was the third country after the Soviet Union and the U.S. that carried out a soft landing on the moon, capturing global attention.

According to the list of global top 500 super computers, with computing speed of 36880 teraflops per second, Tianhe-2 developed by National University of Defense Technology became the fastest super computer in the world.

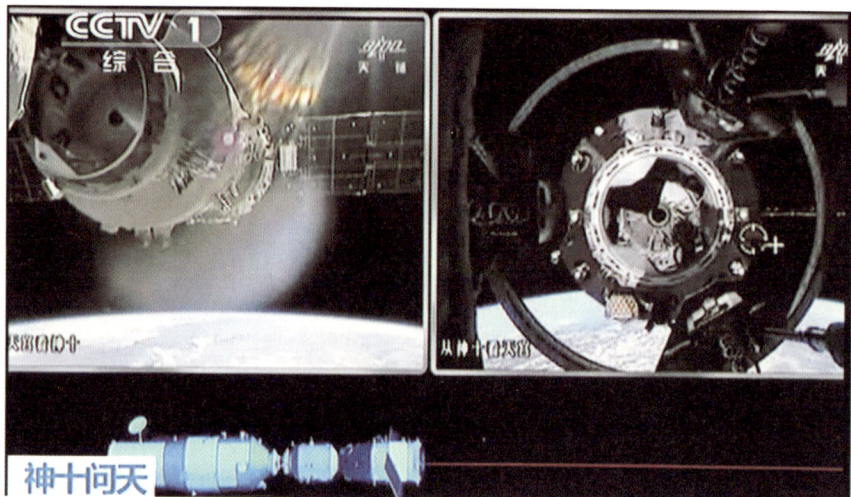

At 10:07 on June 23rd, 2013, under accurate operation of astronaut Nie Haisheng and close cooperation of astronaut Zhang Xiaoguang and Wang Yaping, manual control docking was successfully made between Tiangong-1 target aircraft and Shenzhou-10 spaceship.

In November 2010, the National University of Defense Technology developed the "Tianhe-1" super computer with measured computing speed of 2.57 quadrillion computations per second. Its speed was first in the world. In the latest list of 500 top global super computers publicized in June 2013, the "Tianhe-2" came out on top with a floating point computing speed of 33.86 quadrillion computations per second.

On November 8, 2011, the first Mars probe "Yinghuo-1" in China's Mars Exploration Program was launched with a sample-returning probe from Russia, which began to detect and research the Mars surface. On June 27, 2012, China's "Jiaolong" deep-sea manned submersible achieved a maximum depth of 7026 meters in a 7000-meter sea trial, which set up a record in manned submergence.

The development of China's manned space program represents the development level of China's science and technology. In 1992, China's manned

On June 20th, 2013, Wang Yaping "taught in space".

space program was launched. On December 15, 2003 which was 11 years later, China's astronaut Yang Liwei appeared in space. On September 27, 2008, less than five years later, the door of orbital cabin of Shenzhou-7 manned spacecraft opened and China's astronaut Zhai Zhigang did a spacewalk, which saw China emerge as the third country to master space walk technology. In June 2012, manned spacecraft Shenzhou-9 and the target aircraft Tiangong-1 finished the rendezvous and docking successfully for the first time. In June 2013, China's astronauts Nie Haisheng, Zhang Xiaoguang and Wang Yaping on the manned spacecraft Shenzhou-10 completed the automatic and manual rendezvous and docking with the target aircraft Tiangong-1, which consolidated the technology of rendezvous and docking. Female astronaut WangYaping also gave lectures to tens of millions of Chinese students in space.

From the first man-made satellite "Dongfanghong" which was launched successfully on April 24th, 1970 to Shenzhou-10, China's aerospace industry became stronger and stronger over 43 years. Narrowing the gap between China and top level internationally, China completed the transformation from follower to leader.

The China Manned Space Engineering Office has announced that China's manned engineering will enter into a new phase of manned space station construction. The Tiangong-2 laboratory will be launched around 2015, while the test core cabin of the space station will be launched in 2018 and China's manned space station will be established around 2020. In September 2013, the chief engineer of China's manned space flight, Zhou Jianping, said in an interview with Xinhua that China would like to provide nations and regions looking to peacefully use outer space with opportunities for science experiments and technical tests, so foreign astronauts may land in China's space station.

Development of Science and Technology as a Strong Support of China's Economy and Society

The main value that Chinese science and technology adhere to is to "innovate science and technology, serve the country and benefit people". Science and technology are internationally competitive in the industry of integrated circuit high-end manufacturing equipment and have established a mobile communications industry chain with independent intellectual property rights. The development of a series of strategic new industries, such as biomedicine, energy conservation and environmental protection, new energy, new material and information network, has become the new economic growth point. Enterprises have been the subject of technological innovation. In 2013,

In the building of Lenovo Group (China) Ltd. in Beijing.

the sales revenue of Chinese high-tech industries broke the record of RMB 11 trillion. From the aspect of the internal structure of manufacturing industries, the added value of high-tech manufacturing increased 12.2% in 2012, 2.2% higher than the industrial growth of designated size. The technological content of industrial manufacturing has improved.

Liu Chuanzhi and Lenovo are representatives of Chinese science-and-technology enterprises. With 11 employees and RMB 200,000 Liu started from a small house in Zhongguancun. With continuous innovation and development, Lenovo now owns more than 11,000 global patents, including more than 7000 patents produced by Chinese businesses and more than 4000 patents produced by foreign businesses. In 2005, Lenovo finished the acquisition of IBM's global personal computer business. In the second quarter of 2013, the global market share of Lenovo reached 16.7%, which exceeded HP and became the No. 1 global PC Company. As many as 29 million Lenovo products were sold in one quarter, which meant 4 units every second. Its business volume exceeded RMB 34 billion with business in more than 160 countries, which marked its rise to the peak of the industry.

Science and technology have made tremendous contributions to agricultural growth. As a developing populous country, China faces the problems of arable land shortages, water stress and frequent and repeated disasters. In order to solve the problem of food safety, China, on the basis of key breakthroughs in aspects of rice molecular design breeding and the optimized cultivation theory of biodiversity, has established a modern agricultural technology system of grain crops including rice, wheat and corn. Chinese corn hybrid has been upgraded twice in 10 years and 100-mu of super hybrid rice experimental plot developed by Yuan Longping has set a new record with production of 988 kilograms per mu. The national coverage rate of improved seeds has exceeded 95%, which not only ensures food safety in China but also maintains the stability of the international grain market. The

Development and Innovation of Science and Technology, Philosophy and Social Sciences

On February 28th, 2008, special ceremony of the 30th anniversary of China-UK alliance in science and technology was held in Shanghai Science and Technology Museum. Science and Technology Department of British Council Shanghai Office and British Council signed MOU with Shanghai Science and Technology Committee.

hybrid rice technology developed by Yuan Longping has been extended to more than 20 countries, bringing hope to the solution of hunger in the world.

As for transportation, in 2006 China solved three global engineering problems of frozen earths, alpine hypoxia and ecological fragility and completed the Qinghai-Tibet Railway, the highest and longest rail line in the world. In September 2010, the trial operation of the Shanghai-Hangzhou Railway was carried out. With a maximum speed of 416.6 kilometers, it set a world speed record.

Chen Hualan, director of China's national avian influenza reference laboratory, was elected into the 2013 Top Ten Scientific Figures in *Nature* magazine for helping tackle H9N9 avian influenza. *Nature* named her the "influenza detective".

During the course of scientific and technological development, China benefited from the Soviet Union and western countries with advanced science and technology. In 1978, the Chinese Academy of Sciences and the Royal Society of the UK signed a cooperation agreement on science and technology and a long-term and stable communicative and cooperative relation was established, which helped cultivate many talents for the Chinese Academy of Sciences. Queen Elizabeth II announced the foundation of the "royal scholarship program" and 30 excellent Chinese young scientists were sponsored to travel to the UK and do post doctoral research. Now as the largest developing country in the world, besides continuously promoting cooperation with scientific research units in aspects of scientific and technological cooperation, talent cultivation, scientific research exchanges and joint scientific research institution establishment, China always pays attention to cooperation with developing countries. In 2013, the Chinese Academy of Sciences started and implemented the "science and education cooperation development project for developing countries". Its targets was to cultivate more than 2000 high-level innovative scientific talents for developing countries by 2020, support preferentially about 10 TWAS Chinese outstanding centers and built around 10 overseas scientific and educational bases. The first plan was to cultivate more than 140 doctoral candidates for developing countries every year.

China has made remarkable achievements in the development of science and technology of China, however, because of its short development history, and complex system, science and technology is not so strong overall and some core technologies still depend on foreign countries. According to the World Bank in 2009, there was a US$ 10 billion deficit in the aspect of intellectual property. China needs to further reform the science and technology system, promote the combination of science and technology and the development of the economy and society, do a perspective layout for a new scientific and technical revolution and an industrial revolution and cultivate more innovative talents.

Prosperity and Development of Philosophy and Social Sciences

China boasts a quite long acadmic tradition. At the beginning of the New China, the philosophy and social science research department is just a part of Chinese Academy of Sciences. Chinese Academy of Social Sciences was established in 1977. During a fairly long time, natural science had been prevailing. Since the access of the new century, the fundamental effect of philosophy and social sciences has attracted people's eyeballs.

In November 2002, the 16th National Congress of Chinese Communist Party proposed paying equal attention to social sciences and natural sciences and give full play to philosophy and social sciences in the development of

Chinese Academy of Social Sciences is a research authority in philosophy and social science.

economy and society. In 2003, the Third Plenary Session of the 16th Central Committee of Chinese Communist Party formally put forward *Establishing the Innovation System of the Theory of Philosophy and Social Sciences* and drew the conclusion that the research ability and results of philosophy and social sciences are important parts of the comprehensive national strength. In June 2006, China issued for the first time *The 11th Five-year Plan of National Philosophy and Social Science Research*. In October 2007, the 17th National Congress of Chinese Communist Party clearly demanded the prospering and developing philosophy and social sciences and promoting the innovation of scientific systems, academic views and research methods. The National 12th Five-year (2011–2015) Plan Outline came up with ideas of giving great impetus to the construction of an innovative system of philosophy and social sciences, the implementation of an innovative project of philosophy and social sciences and prosperity and the development of philosophy and social sciences. The 6th Plenary Session of the 17th Central Committee of Communist Party of China took prosperity and development of philosophy and social sciences as an important part of constructing a socialist cultural power and clearly indicated that philosophy and social sciences should better play the role of learning from world, inheriting civilization, innovating theories, helping govern the country and serving the society. A series of major initiatives show that the prosperity and the development of philosophy and social sciences become national strategy in the development of socialism with Chinese characteristics.

So far China has made progress developing philosophy and social sciences in the following aspects:

Based on the key link of construction of a scientific system and teaching material, the comparatively complete teaching material system of philosophy and social sciences and scientific system with complete range and reasonable layout have been formed. There have been more than 20 first-level disciplines and more than 400 second-level disciplines of philosophy and social sciences and the research system has been built, which focuses on basic research, focuses on the macroscopic strategic countermeasure research and takes comprehensive research as specialty. It should be based on discipline construction, cultivate and train qualified persons and establish an academic research team. So far there have been nearly 400,000 teaching and scientific research persons in philosophy and social sciences with intermediate professional titles or above, in which there have been more than 100,000 persons with senior professional titles. Also there have been more than 30,000 full-time researchers. All these people provide support for the prosperity and development of philosophy and social sciences.

Strengthen the intensity of financial aid for scientific research. In 1999, a social science fund was built to subsidize research all over the country for social science research projects. The total fund has increased to RMB 1.2

On March 21st, 2011, Yu Yongding, member of Chinese Academy of Social Sciences and researcher of Economy and Politics Research Institute of Chinese Academy of Social Sciences was making speech on China Development Forum held by Development Research Center of the State Council.

billion in 2012 from RMB 5 million at the very beginning. It has sponsored 4580 projects covering all disciplines of philosophy and social sciences.

Carry out foreign academic exchanges and cooperation. Chinese academics have established long-term stable exchange and cooperative relations with many international organizations, research institutions, academic societies, universities, foundations and departments of governments. Some scholars expressed their opinions in famous international academic institutions and forums, took part in the agenda design, played an important role in issues of international financial management and international climate negotiations and offered many research results and suggestions with great value to maintain national security and core benefits. Many foreign language periodicals including *Social Sciences in China* (English edition), *China & World Economy*, *Chinese Archaeology*, and *China Economist* have become important channels for China to communicate with the social and scientific fields in the world.

By carrying out innovative project of philosophy and social sciences, China has established the main carrier and platform of an innovative system of philosophy and social sciences, to promote the innovation of a scientific system, academic views, research methods and organization methods of scientific research. Also China focuses on communication and cooperation among different disciplines of philosophy and social sciences and philosophy and social sciences and natural sciences, in order to achieve important comprehensive innovative results and construct the way for theoretical research with Chinese characteristics and academic innovation. Since the start of the innovative projects of philosophy and social sciences in 2002, Chinese Academy of Social Sciences has produced more than 700 academic monographs, 9000 papers, over 3000 research reports and nearly 1000 academic materials, collations of ancient books and textbooks with many high-quality works which have deep influence at home and abroad. For example, in 2013, the pioneering achievements in the fields of philosophy and social

Adunqiaolu rock paintings were located in Bortala Mongol Autonomous Prefecture in Xinjiang Uygur Autonomous Region. According to research, the paintings were finished between the Spring and Autumn Period and the Warring State Period (about 770 B.C.-221 B.C.).

sciences cover *Draft of History of People's Republic of China* (5 volumes), *History of Republic of China* (36 volumes), *National Historical Atlas of People's Republic of China* (1st volume), *A History of Eastern Philosophy* (5 volumes) and *History of Shang Dynasty* (11 volumes) which filled voids in the academic world. Although the book, *Achievements and Significance of Early Bronze Age Sites and Archaeology and Excavations of Graves in Adunqiaolu of Wenquan County in Xinjiang Province*, is not a masterpiece, it is quite important for bronze culture research of Euro-Asia grassland.

In the aspect of providing decisions and countermeasures for the main problems, *Beyond the Demographic Dividend* shows the decisions and answers of how to cope with the appearance of the Lewis Turning-point and the disappearance of the demographic dividend. *International Financial System: Reform and*

Reconstruction follows the international financial crisis, systematically analyzes the evolution of international financial system, issues and trends and explains the policy choice of China. The N*ational Balance Sheet and Risk Assessment* analyzes the national debt problems and gives policy suggestions, which has been quoted by International Monetary Fund and famous investment banks at home and abroad.

However, the discourse system of Chinese philosophy and social sciences is still inadequate. With incomplete overall influence, it does not match economic and social development, and it is not suitable for China's international standing. As the constant depth of the Reform and Opening-up and the continuously expansion of foreign academic exchanges, the peaceful rise of China has become a hot topic and global vision, spirit of the age and national standpoint should be the characteristics of Chinese academic culture. Chinese scholars are devoting themselves to the construction of a discourse system for philosophy and social sciences, which will analyze Chinese problems, explain Chinese views and predict the future of China with Chinese theory and discourse.

A Sound and Orderly Development of Religious Culture

As a country with numerous ethnic groups and religions, China features an inclusive and all-embacing culture. In the situation of unity with diversity, Buddhism, Taoism, Islam, Catholicism and Christianity coexist and make up the diverse religious culture in China. Chinese religious followers and practicioners have the tradition of loving the country and their respective religions. The Chinese government advocates freedom of religious belief, supports and encourages religious organizations to actively take part in the construction of the modern state. Mutual respect, mutual learning and harmonious co-existence are all promoted between religions and the public, between different religions and between different sects in a religion. Thus, in contemporary China, religion sees a sound and orderly development.

Contemporary China's Culture

Respect the Freedom of Religious Belief

The Common Program of the Chinese People's Political Consultative Conference promulgated at the founding of New China regulates that the ethnic groups will have freedom of religious belief. In 1952, when meeting with the Tibetan Delegation, Mao Zedong stressed, "The Communist Party has adopted a policy of protecting religions. Believers and non-believers, believers of one religion or another, are all similarly protected, and their faiths are respected. Today, we have adopted this policy of protecting religions, and in future we will still maintain this policy of protection."

Chinese religious policies are related with the diverse religious traditions of the nation. Since ancient times, China has centered on humanistic beliefs

Corner of temple complex on Mont Wutai, head of Chinese Four Buddhist Holy Mountains, located in Shanxi Province.

A sound and orderly development of religious culture

and governed the country with Confucian theories on benevolence and rites as the core, Buddist and Taoist thoughts as the support and other religions as the supplement. Under the leadership and influence of the Confucian moral reason, religions are in a subordinate position. Max Weber called Chinese Confucianism "a sober religion". Taoism, a religion born in China, has a history of over 1700 years. Buddhism, introduced to China from India over 2000 years ago, gradually combined with Confucianism and Taoism. The combination of Confucianism, Buddhism and Taoism, together with folk beliefs, constitutes the basic genealogy of Chinese religions.

After landing China, foreign religions received edification of Chinese culture and started successive programs of localization. Buddhism peacefully spread to China, successfully merged into Chinese culture and became one of the three pillars for Chinese traditional culture with Confucianism and Taoism. Catholicism was introduced to China in the 7th century and Christianity (Protestantism) in 1807. Western religions often contradicted Chinese traditional culture and were not recognized in China for a long time. In the period under the reign of Emperor Kangxi in the Qing Dynasty, the rites controversy broke out due to the Roman Curia's disallowance of its Chinese followers to respect Confucianism and ancestors and caused the ban of Catholicism in China for a century. When Christianity spread to China on a large scale, "all missionaries have won benefits and advantages from the Opium War and the treaties and decrees signed with the defeated China in the war." (Port White) Educator Jiang Menglin once said, "The Buddha rides a white elephant to China, while the Jesus Christ flies to China on bullets." In early 20th century, Christianism and Catholicism ran schools, especially universities, in China, which changed the situation to some degree. Many Chinese Christians proposed to create China Protestant Independence Society beyond the jurisdiction of western churches. After the founding of New China, Chinese Christianity carried out the "self-management, self-maintenance and self-missionizing" renovation movement, opened the door for Christianity's

Wangfujing Catholic Church built in 1655 is one of the four major Catholic churches in Beijing, whose original name was St. Joseph Cathedral, also called East Church or Eight Side Slot Church.

development in China, realized the unified churches and localization of Christianity, and integrated the religion into Chinese culture. In August 1957, Catholicism established Chinese Patriotic Catholic Followers Association (later renamed as Chinese Patriotic Catholic Association) consisting of bishop, priest and church members.

China boasts diverse religions in multiple-levels. In addition to five major religions, there are ethnic religions, folk religions and folk-custom religions. Some people of Zhuang, Yao, Bai, Yi, Jing and Mulam ethnic groups believe in Taoism. The people of Tibetan, Mongolian, Tu and Yugur ethnic groups profess Lamaism. Some people of Dai, Blang, De'ang, Achang, Jingpo and Lahu ethnic groups believe in Hinayana Buddhism. Islam is the core religious belief of ten ethinic groups, such as Uygur, Hui, Kazak, Kirgiz, Tatar, Ozbek, Tajik, Dongxiang, Salar and Bonan. Some people of Russian and Ewenki ethnic groups profess to be of the Eastern Orthodox faith. Shamanism is believed in

A sound and orderly development of religious culture

by some people of Daur, Oroqen and Ewenki ethnic groups. Some primitive religions are maintained or kept by ethnic groups. The diversity of religions brings China the title of "a united nations of religions." Despite some small skirmishes between religions, harmonious and peaceful religious relationship has been the overwhelming result of such diversity.

With the founding of New China, Chinese religious circles took an important step in adapting to modern society and culture, by means of democratic system's reform and independent church operation. Article 88 of the *Constitution of the People's Republic of China* definitely regulates: "The citizens of the People's Republic of China have freedom of religious belief." The Constitution defines that freedom of religious belief is the basic right of citizens, religions can meet people's spiritual demand and should not be disturbed if they don't hinder politics, economy and production. Thus, the world outlook and political stand of religious followers are separated. Chinese people often regard religion as a part of culture and religious culturalism is widely accepted by the public. Religious culture originates from and nourishes secular culture.

In the 1950s, the CPC Central Committee enacted religion policies with the main contents as follow. First, the citizens have freedom of religious belief and disbelief. Second, religions will uphold their basic beliefs and doctrines and maintain religious systems and rites consistent with their characteristics. Third, religions will independently carry out regular religious activities within the scope authorized in the Constitution, laws and policies. Fourth, all religions are equal under the law of the PRC and atheists and theists should respect each other. Finally, that religious bodies and religious affairs are not subject to any foreign domination. These policies have been applied to date.

As in all other nations, in China, religious bodies have their own organizations. Nationwide religious bodies include the Buddhist Association of China, the Taoist Association of China, the Islamic Association of China,

Contemporary China's Culture

Delegation from the religious circles during the "two sessions" in 2013.

Chinese Patriotic Catholic Association, Bishops' Conference of Catholic Church in China, National Committee of Three-Self Patriotic Movement of the Protestant Churches in China and China Christian Council. The religious bodies elect their leaders and leading organs in accordance with their constitutions. In addition, representatives from religious circles have attended all previous sessions of Chinese People's Political Consultative Conference (CPPCC) and National People's Congress (NPC). The act of attending the CPPCC and NPC meetings evokes the patriotic enthusiasm and initiative to build socialism of both senior religious personae and numerous religion believers.

A sound and orderly development of religious culture

The Positive Role of Religions in Promoting Social Harmony

In the transitionary period from the 1970s to the 1980s, China recovered the churches and other religious places damaged during the Cultural Revolution, carried out the policy of freedom of religious belief, and examined religions from a new view angle. In April 4, 1980, Deng Xiaoping published *A Significant Event* in *People's Daily* to sufficiently affirm religious personae's active role in international cultural exchanges through commemorating the Tang Dynasty's dignitary Jianzhen. Furthermore, in the 1990s, China brought

Seda Buddhist College located in Seda County in Garze Tibetan Autonomous Prefecture, Sichuan Province.

forward the concept of "actively guiding religions to adapt to socialist society", not only deepening the understanding to religions' positive functions in the new era and the diversity of socialist culture but also defining a new relationship between politics and religions.

In the new century, China has furthered its comprehensive understanding to the natural, social, recognitive and psychological sources of religions. Religion is not only a world outlook and spiritual force but also a long and pervasive social force in the world community. Religious relation is one of the five social relations (party relations, ethnic relations, religious relations, strata relation, and domestic and overseas compatriot relation) concerning the nation's overall situation in social political life. Efforts are to be made in giving play to religion's active role in boosting social harmony, encouraging and supporting religious personae to promote the good tradition of loving the country and religion, uniting together for progress and serving for the society. In addition, the government will help religious groups by supporting them to make contributions for national unity, economic development, social progress, social harmony and national reunification, and assisting them to construe the creeds in a way compliant with social progress.

As a culture system based on a central belief, religion is special. However, as a social organization, religion should abide by the secular rules and cannot outmatch social order. China has actively boosted legalized and standardized management of religious affairs. The Constitution of the PRC amended in 1982 further standardized the citizen's freedom of religious belief. In Article 36, it clearly says:

"Citizens of the People's Republic of China enjoy freedom of religious belief. No state organ, public organization or individual may compel citizens to believe in, or not to believe in, any religion; nor may they discriminate against citizens who believe in, or do not believe in, any religion. The state protects normal religious activities. No one may make use of religion to engage

A sound and orderly development of religious culture

in activities that disrupt public order, impair the health of citizens or interfere with the educational system of the state."

In November 2004, the State Council promulgated *Regulations on Religious Affair*, marking a new stage in the legal development of religious affairs, that the government will safeguard the standardized and orderly operation of religious activities, and meanwhile, severely crack down the separatist activities, delinquencies and crimes under the veil of religion. The *Rules for the Implementation of Administrative Licensing Items related with Religious Affairs* amended in 2012 actively boosted the government's power to administer by law and standardize administration of religious affairs.

Over the thirty years since the beginning of the process of reform and opening-up, Chinese religious bodies have independently handled their own affairs, established religious schools, printed, published and circulated religious

On January 28th, 2011, Joint Declaration of Religious Harmony was made by five major national religious groups of China at National People's Congress Center. Photo of delegators taken after the meeting.

classics and periodicals and undertaken social welfare services. Temples and chapels have been built in many communities while infrastructures like roads and pipelines cover religious places. Religious followers enjoy equal treatment with citizens including basic social guarantees like pension and medical insurances, and perform the duties and obligations of citizens. After investigating the living status of Tibetan monks and nuns, American scholar John Naisbitt wrote, "The Central Government pays monthly salary to the clergy. They are supplied with food, clothing, and even mobile phones. Perhaps they also enjoy the Internet access for information communication and activity coordination."

The government helps religious bodies and schools to improve the office and school's conditions. In 2006, the new campus of Chinese Catholic Academy of Theology and Philosophy was founded and put into use. Covering an area of 4.67 hectares with an overall floorage of 20,168 square meters, the academy, boasting complete facilities and 24 Chinese and foreign professors, is one of the catholic schools with a high modernization and the highest teaching level in Asia. In turn, Christianity has about 55,000 chapels and mass sites in China, of which 70% are new ones, and the biggest assembly area can hold 7000 worshippers.

The performance of freedom of religious belief offers a relaxed social environment for religion's development in China. The profound social reform and the diversification of people's thoughts bring new development potential for religions and a great increase of followers. According to incomplete statistics, China has more than 100 million believers of various religions, accounting for about 10% of the total population, about 360,000 clergies and 140,000 legally registered and opened religious sites, generally meeting the demands of followers, and 5500 religious groups with orderly religious activities. China has also recovered and built 97 religious schools, and set up a complete religious school education system in general. By 2012, China has

A sound and orderly development of religious culture

printed more than 100 million copies of *Bibles* and become one of the countries with the most *Bibles* printed. Chinese religious circles keeps exchanges with religious bodies in more than 70 countries and regions. By April 2012, China had held three sessions of World Buddhist Forum. Religious personages take an active part in the politics, and 17,000 of them are members of the NPC or CPPCC.

Buddhism has the most followers and greatest influence among five most influential religions in China. China has more than 13,000 Buddhist temples, about 200,000 monks and nuns. Of which, the Tibetan Language Buddhism has about 120,000 Lamas and nuns, more than 1700 living Buddhas, more than 3000 temples, and about 7.5 million followers. The Pali Language Buddhism has nearly 10,000 Bhiksu and monks, and more than 1600 temples. In addition to the increase of converts, the Chinese Language Buddhism has numerous devout lay Buddhists. Taiwan's religionist and philanthropist Master Hsing Yun is fairly venerable in ethnic Chinese. He has more than 1000 monachal

On November 5th, 2013, Grand Master Hsing Yun from Taiwan Province gave the speech "Seeing the Power of Dream" at Sun Yatsen Memorial Hall in Guangzhou.

disciples, more than 260 training sites, 9 galleries, 50-plus Chinese language schools and 16 Buddhist institutes across the world. The schools and institutes focus on humanity, art and Buddhism.

All of China's religions are secularized ones with realistic significance. Buddist bodies strive to discover and promote religious doctrines and morals in favor of social development, progress and civilization. Traditional Buddhist rules promote Six Harmony and Respect, i.e. six principles of Buddhists. The Six Harmony and Respect, with the core values of harmony, can be deemed as the Buddist commandments for keeping harmony or the Buddist attitude in conducts. In April 2006, the Mount Putuo Declaration was announced at the First World Buddhism Forum held in the famous southern Buddist spot Mount Putuo, Zhejiang. The Declaration proposed the new Buddhist Six Harmony concept to promote "warm heart, happy family, friendly relationship, peaceful society, harmonious civilization and peaceful world." The new concept

On April 26th, 2012, opening ceremony and keynote speech of the Third World Buddhist Forum were held in the Hong Kong Coliseum. Over 1300 monks from all around the world attended the ceremony of "Thousand Monks Having Lunch Together" at noon.

A sound and orderly development of religious culture

indicates that the core value of Buddhism is Harmony. The forum insisted on the theme of "everyone bears his share of the responsibility for a harmonious world; and the harmonious world originates from the hearts of everyone," fully embodying Chinese religion's support to the world and love to the common people. In 2012, Master Hsing Yun founded Secular Buddhism Institute which, together with Chinese Cultural Research Institute of Nanjing University, jointly held a Symposium on Secular Buddhism's Theory and Practice. At the symposium, Master Hsing Yun said that secular Buddhism is the original Buddhism, happy, peaceful, joyful and equal. He reiterated that Buddhism can purify hearts. He intends to bring harmony and peace for the country and society with Buddhism and utilize Buddhist doctrines to purify hearts and improve morals, ethos and social orders.

Chinese Taoism, with respect to Tao and Virtues as the tenet, has pursued for "*hehe* (harmony)", undertaken the mission of civilizing the people and promoted support to the world and assistance to the people of the nation and other counties. China has more than 1500 Taoist temples and 25,000 Taoist priests. The Muslim population in China had risen to 22 million. China has more than 30,000 mosques and 40,000 imam and ahung.

China Catholicism's chiefs and clergies have upheld the banner of patriotism and Catholicism and insisted on the principle of independence in religious affairs and election of bishops. The number of Chinese Catholics rises from 3 million in the early period of the New China to 5.7 million today. The religion has about 4000 clergies, 4600-plus churchs and sites. China Catholicism plays an active role in international exchanges. Chinese Patriotic Catholic Association has sent 340 priests, friars and sisters to Occidental and Asian countries to learn theology. More than 150 of them have earned PhD or Master Degree and returned back to their parishes and abbeys. Nearly 100 overseas Catholic theologists have been invited to China to give lectures. And dozens of Chinese groups with more than 1000 members have visited the

Catholic Church in 20-plus countries and regions. China Catholicism, with the tenet of "honor the God and help the people with services and devotion", has been devoted to social charity and welfare and encouraged the rural followers to pave the roads, dig wells, open hospitals, clinics and nursing homes and fund the Hope Primary Schools. Between 2000 and 2009, the Catholic chiefs and clergies had donated 100 million yuan for disaster-hit areas, printed and published nearly 10 million copies of various periodicals and books including the Bible and other holy books.

Christianity, has a short history in China and has gradually adapted to Chinese culture after the years. The missionary mode was also localized somehow. Christianity has seen a robust development since the 1990s.

Mosque in Xinjiang.

A sound and orderly development of religious culture

According to incomplete statistics, China has about 23 million Christians, 30 times higher than that (700,000 Christians) in the early period of the New China. Among the five major religions in China, Christianity sees the fastest growth, followed by Buddhism. Followers of Catholicism and Islamism synchronize with the natural population growth. The number of Taoists rises comparatively slowly.

In recent years, the structure of religious followers has undergone a dramatic change. First, more and more young and middle-aged people believe in religions, having a continuous rising proportion in population. Second, more urban people believe in religions. Third, occupations of believers are more diverse. Four, folk beliefs, once declined in history, come back in some regions. In the transition of Chinese society, religion becomes a barrier for disadvantageous groups to resist psychological pressure and plays a supportive function for the normal social operation.

Some religious problems still exist in China. For example, some clergies excessively seek after secular benefits and can't reach a balance between the secular and the spiritual worlds, between the beliefs and self-culture. In addition, domestic and foreign separatist forces attempt to utilize religions to divide the country. They distort religious doctrines, incite discontents, cheat and coerce the people to attend terrorist activities, especially the "Tibetan Separation" and "East Turkestan forces". Some lawbreakers at home and penetrated from abroad established illegal organizations under the cloak of religion, and serevely endangered the normal life of blind people. The government has identified 14 cults. Obviously, these are not the problems of religions.

However, generally speaking, religions play an active role in promoting social harmony in China. When the world is disturbed by "religious fever" and "cultural collision", China has generally achieved the unity and harmony between the people who believe in religions and those who don't, between the people who believe in different religions.

Religious Cultural Situation in Tibet

Nearly all the people of about 20 ethnic groups in China believe in religions. Ten ethnic groups in Xinjiang believe in Islamism. Religion is pervasive in Tibet, a place worthy of its name "religious land". Nearly all Tibetans believe in religion and Tibetan religious status is often discussed in western reports on human rights. Then, how about the reality in Tibet?

In May 1951, the eve of the peaceful liberation of Tibet, the Central Government stressed, "efforts will be made in carrying out the policy of freedom of religious belief, respecting the religious belief and customs of Tibetans, and developing Tibetan language, words and school education." In 1953, the 14th Dalai and the 10th Panchen were elected honorary chairmen of the Buddhist Association of China, and the Kun Bde Gling Living Buddha

On April 1st of the Tibetan calendar is Saga Dawa, a traditional Tibetan festival.

A sound and orderly development of religious culture

was elected vice chairman of the Buddhist Association of China. In September 1954, the 14th Dalai and the 10th Panchen attended 1st session of the First National People's Congress (NPC) of the PRC in Beijing, and the 14th Dalai was elected vice chairman of the NPC. At the congress, based on his observation and experience in the previous several years, Dalai Lama said, "the rumor that 'the Party and the People's government destroy religions' has come to naught. Tibetans have experienced the freedom of religious belief by themselves." In September 1956, Tibetan Branch of the Buddhist Association of China was established.

Tibet has 1787 religious sites with more than 46,000 monks and nuns, and 358 living Buddhas. Most followers set up a sutra hall or a Buddha shrine at their homes. Buddhists, laymen and followers hold and attend various religious and traditional activities, such as the Sa Gada Watt Festival. Each year, more than a million believers arrived in Lhasa to worship the Buddha. The reincarnation of living Buddha, the special succession mode of Tibetan Buddhism, received full respect. Traditional religious activities including learning sutras, discussing sutras, initiation, abhisenca and practices, together with sutra examinations and academic degree promotions, are held normally. Various rituals are held on occasion of major religious festivals. Reincarnation of living Buddha, a special succession rite in Tibetan Buddhism, receives respect of the Central Government. Since the democratic reform, more than 60 reincarnated living Buddha have been verified and approved in accordance with historical rules and religious procedures.

In 2010, British reporter Brandon O'Neal visited Tibet, and then published an article in American newspaper *Christian Science Monitor* on July 29, reading, "When you first arrived in Tibet, the freedom of religious belief enjoyed by Tibetans will impress you deeply. Activists of Free Tibet in the UK said that Chinese authority attempted to 'eliminate Tibetan identity and culture'. However, when I see Tibetans can nearly be free in religious rites every day, I feel surprising and gratified. " French reporter Maxime Vivas

On June 9th, 2007, Tripitaka printed in North Song Dynasty (960–1127) was first exhibited to the public on Papermaking and Printing Fair held by the National Library in Beijing.

said, "As an atheist, I felt extremely surprising when I saw numerous Tibetan Buddhist temples and clergies in the street (in our atheist world, we never tolerate so many priests)."

In order to cultivate senior talents on Tibetan Buddhism, the 10th Panchen Lama hosted the founding of the High-Level Tibetan Buddhism College of China in 1987. Over the past 26 years, groups of dignitaries, including students from Geluk, Nyingma, Sakya, Kargyu and Jonang sects have earned the senior academic degree Tuo Ran Ba. Tibetan Buddhism College is established in Lhasa to nurture Buddhism talents locally. The country protects Tibetan religious cultural heritages and passes on Tibetan culture.

At the beginning of the peaceful liberation of Tibet, the Central Government stressed, "Efforts will be made in protecting cultural relics, historic sites, Buddha statues/pictures, Buddhist sutras, pagodas and instruments inside temples, protecting and fixing sutra halls, Buddha halls and houses for temples." In June 1959, the Working Committee of CPC Tibetan Committee issued *Decisions on Strengthening Cultural Heritages Archiving*, established

A sound and orderly development of religious culture

Cultural Relics and Historic Sites Archiving Management Committee of the Working Committee of CPC Tibetan with a subordinated Cultural Heritages Management Group. The Central Government organized the salvage, sorting and publication of lots of religious literatures and classics. *Tibetan Tripitaka* including more than 4500 sutras is the major part of *Tibetan* Buddhist classics. In 1986, the country initiated the "*Tibetan Tripitaka* Collation Project" in China Tibetology Research Center, established a collation bureau for the project in Chengdu, Sichuan and appointed a group of erudite scholars to collate all editions related. The year of 2011 witnessed the completion of the enormous project: a total of 4570 sutras in 232 volumes were all published by China Tibetology Press. The collation and sorting of *Tibetan Tripitaka*, first of its kind in history, not only effectively protects Tibetan traditional culture, but also contributes to show the similarities and differences between the Han's and Tibetan Buddhism as well as their historical origins.

On April 12th, 2014, in Dengfeng, Shi Yong Xin, head of the Shaolin Temple led his disciples to greet the full edition of *Tripitaka* at gate to their temple. The *Tripitaka* will be consecrated in the temple.

Contemporary China's Culture

On April 16th, 2014, exhibition of "Niangben's Tibetan Thang-ga Painting" was held in China National Museum.

The sutra printing houses of temples also continue to print sutras and have been expanded in recent years. Nearly 60 traditional sutra printing houses are attached to the Muru Temple, the Potala Palace and other temples print 63,000 kinds of sutra volumes each year. The sutras are sold in 20 nongovernmental stalls. Meanwhile, the preservation of active temples focuses on cultural heritage protection. Over a long period, the country invested a quantity of funds in maintaining the temples in Tibet, protecting and fixing religion culture's carriers like murals, sculptures, statues, Thangka, sutras, instruments and shrines in temples. Between 1989 and 1994, the country allocated a special fund of 53 million yuan, gold and silver and other noble materials in the first protective maintenance to the Potala Palace. Between 2001 and 2010,

A sound and orderly development of religious culture

maintenances were made to key cultural heritages including the Jokhang Temple, the Sekhar-Guthog Temple, the Tashihunpo Temple, the Shalu Temple and the Ramoche Temple. In the new century, the country has invested 2.04 billion yuan in protecting Tibetan cultural heritages, including 38 million yuan earmarked for the maintenance of three major heritages, i.e. the Potala Palace (the 2nd-phase maintenance), the Norulingka and Sayi Temple. The Potala Palace, the Jokhang Temple and the Norulingka are inscribed in the UNESCO World Cultural Heritages.

Today, Tibet is home to 4277 cultural heritage sites including three World Cultural Heritages, two Humankind Intangible Cultural Heritages, 55 National Primary Cultural Heritages, 76 National Intangible Cultural Heritages, 224 Autonomous Region-level Cultural Heritages, and 323 Autonomous Region-level Intangible Cultural Heritages. The ancient, mysterious and religion-related intangible cultural heritages, such as Thangka, Tibetan incense, Tibetan paper and Lhasa Sho Dun Festival, are displayed and showcase their enchanting traditions. In 2013, the cultural, sports and media expenditures of Tibet hit 2373.98 million yuan including 232.71 million yuan in cultural heritage protection and 117.42 million yuan in supporting literature creation, intangible cultural heritage protection and development of grassroots culture and cultural facilities.

In order to pass on Tibetan intangible cultural heritages to the young generation, the Lhasa municipal government has appointed renowned professors of Tibet University to compile regional textbooks documenting such intangible cultural heritage. The textbooks were recently published and popularized in Lhasa schools to give the children basic knowledge on and sense of protection of the local cultural heritages.

The Tibetan-dominant bilingual education is carried out in Tibetan education system. At the end of 2012, in Tibet, a total of 282,914 pupils and 177,981 high school students studied in bilingual primary and high schools, accounting for 96.88% and 90.63% of the totals respectively. Now Tibet has 23,085 bilingual teachers and 3700 dedicated Tibetan teachers.

In addition, Tibetans' cultural rights are also respected by the government. Tibet has 14 Tibetan magazines and 10 Tibetan newspapers. Tibetan People's Broadcast Station has 42 Tibetan (including the Khampa language) programs, 21-hour-long Tibetan news and 18-hour-long Khampa program per day. The Tibetan Satellite TV of Tibet TV Station airs programs around the clock. In 2012, Tibet Autonomous Region published 780 kinds of Tibetan books with a total impression of 4.31 million copies. Tibetan is China's first ethnic group's character with the international coding standard for information interchange. Thus, Tibetan speakers can proceed without hindrance into the information technology era.

International Influence of Chinese Culture

In order to strengthen the world's understanding to Chinese culture, a multi-level, multi-discipline and all-round cultural exchange pattern has been set up by means of governmental and non-governmental efforts, cultural exchanges and trading affairs, parallel operation of "going global" and "ushering into China." In addition, establishment of Confucius institutes in foreign countries, together with other methods, are applied to reinforce international publicity, boost export of cultural products and services, expand cultural enterprises' international investment and multinational operation, and enhance Chinese culture's international influence.

The Presentation of Chinese Culture's "Going Global" Strategy

The continuity and cohesiveness of Chinese traditional culture are not only unmatched in the world, but also make unique contribution to humankind's progress and development. Descriptions on China in *The Travels of Marco Polo* aroused Europeans eagerness to the oriental world. Matteo Ricci translated Confucius classics into Latin. Then the Latin versions were translated into French and German and circulated across the world. In his *Essai sur les moeurs*, French Enlightenment thinker Voltaire wrote, "Let us first pay attention to a nation. The nation has owned a continuous history recorded in a fixed language. European nobilities and merchants discovered the oriental world, but only focused on wealth, while the philosphers developed a new

Head portrait of Voltaire. Beijing Confucius Temple and the Imperial College Museum.

International influence of Chinese culture

spiritual and material world." He praised Chinese culture and created the drama *A Chinese Orphan* to reflect the culture. The renowned French writer Balzac of the 19th century also favored and appreciated Chinese culture. In his full-length novel *Illusions perdues*, Balzac described Chinese papermaking and printing techniques in lengthy paragraphs. He also authored a lengthy paper *China and Chinese* to show his enthusiasm and appreciation to Chinese culture. *Science and Civilisation in China*, written by British natural science history expert Joseph Needham, gives a comprehensive introduction to ancient China's science technology thoughts and status, indicating that Chinese inventions of gun powder, compass and papermaking, and the mathematic concepts offered new thinking and created good opportunities for Europe's initiation of the brand new science technology epoch. He believed that western civilization would not reach the level or reach the level several centuries later if without the contribution of Chinese civilization. In addition, Chinese gardening architecture, garments and customs were imitated by Europeans at that time.

It is well-known that some proposed the "wholesale westernization" with the western culture's input into China. After new China was established, efforts were also made in the area of foreign culture exchange in addition to actively developing the new culture. After the reform and opening-up, China gradually carried out comprehensive foreign cultural exchanges, actively learned and borrowed global cultural achievements, introduced advanced culture and science technology, management concepts and mechanism to enrich Chinese culture. Without the opening-up, contemporary Chinese culture will not have the prosperous development.

However, the cultural differences between China and the West are very evident. Chinese culture praises highly on "*He He* (harmony and coordination)", and emphasizes the integral pursuance for commonness, moderation, benevolence and harmony, which is very different from the Western culture which advocates personal value. The cultural collision between

Contemporary China's Culture

On November 4th, 2013, Training Base of International Promotion of Chinese Language and Food Culture in Hubei University approved by Economics Office of Chinese Language Council International welcomed its first 12 French students who are also members of French Panda Association.

China and West is inevitable due to the differences in cultural backgrounds, social systems, ideologies and ways of thinking as well as the West's unaccustomedness to China's rapid development. Although the economic interdependence between China, an important trade partner of more than 120 countries today, and other countries are continuously increasing, the so-called "China Threat", "Collapse of China" and "China's Global Resource Plunder" are still disseminated through various forms in some countries and regions. Against the backdrop of increasingly intensified cultural exchange, fusion and confrontation, China needs to remedy the insufficient communications in the past, leverage extensive international cultural exchanges to promote mutual understanding and consensus, enhance trust and friendship, especially, strengthen international community's knowledge and understanding to the

International influence of Chinese culture

basic conditions, values, development road as well as domestic and foreign policies of China, and create a favorable international environment for Chinese development. This is the background of the "going global" strategy of Chinese culture.

In 1997, the Central Committee of the CPC brought forward the "going global" strategy of Chinese culture. Upon entry into the 21st century, the cultural consciousness gradually becomes a common understanding. China's entry into the WTO offers a more spacious platform for Chinese culture's presentation to the world. With the continuous development of the Chinese economy, China's comprehensive national strength has been greatly increasing. China further defines the basic ideas and framework. The promulgation of *Opinions concerning Further Strengthening and Improving Cultural Products and Services Export* in July 2005 and *Some Policies on Encouraging and Supporting Cultural Products and Services Export* in 2006 marks the preliminary formation of the "going global" strategy of Chinese culture. In 2010, the Ministry of Culture developed the *2011–2015 Master Plan for Promoting Cultural Products and Services "Going Global"*, elaborated the objectives, tasks and measures for promoting cultural products and services "going global" and dramatically accelerated the pace of Chinese culture's "going global". In November 2012, the 18th National Congress of the CPC reiterated: we should expand opening-up in cultural field, actively absorb and borrow outstanding foreign cultural achievements, and meanwhile, develop Chinese culture in a more open environment and strengthen the self-identity and confidence in national culture.

Enriching Carriers for Cultural Exchanges

Since the beginning of the 21th century, China has maintained comprehensive, multi-level and extensive cultural exchanges with the world, expanded foreign cultural exchanges through government's leadership, enterprises' organizing, marketed operation and public participation, and enriched the carriers for cultural exchanges.

Cultural exchange mechanisms and systems have been established between Chinese and foreign governments to actively carry out various

On June 25th, "Peony Pavilion", a classical kunqu repertoire rehearsed by North Qunqu Opera Theater gave a performance at Pierre Cardin Theater in Paris to celebrate the 50th anniversary of diplomatic relations between China and France.

International influence of Chinese culture

cultural exchanges and systems. Currently, China has maintained good cultural exchanges with more than 160 countries and regions, signed inter-governmental cultural cooperation agreements with 149 countries, and inked more than 800 annual cultural exchange plans with 97 countries. China has also carried out cultural exchanges with nearly 1000 international cultural organizations and institutions, established cultural departments in 100-plus embassies and consulates stationed in 99 countries as well as 14 overseas Chinese cultural centers in Paris, Berlin and Tokyo etc.

With the continuous rise of China-foreign cultural exchanges, China has held various cultural exchange activities, such as Cultural Year, Language Year, Tourism Year, Cultural Festival, Art Festival, Movie Festival and International Book Expo, in many countries, and vice versa. Since the China-France Cultural Year jointly held by both countries in 2003, China has successfully held cultural year events in the UK, the USA, Russia, Italy and India etc. These activities, covering politics, economy, science and technology, culture, art, education and many other fields, helped to deepen the mutual understanding between China and foreign countries, and strengthened the friendship between Chinese and people all over the world. Coinciding with the Beijing 2008 Olympic Games, "Meeting in Beijing–2008", invited nearly 10,000 performance artists from 110 international art organizations of more than 80 countries and regions and received over 3 million in audience, was the most influential international cultural exchange since the founding of New China and is an excellent example of the Culture-centered Olympics. Each year, about 50 Chinese movie shows (weeks) are held out of China to exhibit more than 400 Chinese films. Chinese filmmakers have more and more opportunities to showcase their works at the film festivals of Berlin, Hollywood and Cannes. Quite a few Chinese films won awards at important international film festivals.

Currently, there are plentiful carriers for China's foreign cultural exchanges. The representatives are as follows.

Confucius Institute

Language is a big barrier for Chinese culture's "going global". Thus, China carried out the Confucius Institute development plan which focuses on language teaching and promotion. On November 21, 2004, China unveiled the world's first nonprofitable education organization Confucius Institute in Seoul, Republic of Korea. So far, China has established 440 Confucius institutes and 646 Confucius classes with 850,000 registered students across more than 120 countries. Each year, China sent about 10,000 Chinese teachers and volunteers to these institutes for the teaching work. Confucius Institute Headquarters has published core textbooks in 45 languages, distributed 12 million textbooks to 136 countries and helped these countries to compile localized teaching materials. In 2009, Confucius Institute Headquarters started to publish bilingual *Confucius Institute Bimonthly* in eight languages. Confucius Institute Online is available in 46 languages and accessible for registered users from 125 countries. Meanwhile, Confucius Institute Headquarters actively carried out cultural exchange activities, organized Chinese Bridge Mandarin Contest with participants of college and high school students, held nearly 10,000 activities including cultural and art tour shows, textbook tour exhibitions and tour lectures of famous teachers with above 5 million participants, and invited foreign education officials, teachers and students to visit China and experience Chinese culture. Then Confucius Institute is an important institution for the international spread of Chinese, a bridge for the expansion of China-foreign friendship, and a window for the world to know China.

In addition to selecting teachers and volunteers from nationwide schools, the Confucius Institute also nurtures local faculty and has trained 100,000 Chinese teachers for more than 80 countries. It helps local teachers to have a deep understanding to Chinese culture, offers pertinent high-quality textbooks for people with different cultural backgrounds and targeted demands, strengthens interactive with foreign Sinological institutions, and encourages

International influence of Chinese culture

On April 28th, 2014, Chinese Culture Day activities were held at Bordeaux College of Business Administration in Dakar, capital of Senegal. During the activities, students and faculties had a distinctive fashion show wearing cloths of Chinese minority nationalities.

social organizations, agencies and overseas Chinese to attend the institute construction and cultural exchange projects and enrich the activities of the institute.

Altogether 42 countries and regions have included Chinese into their national education system. The number of Chinese learners has rapidly risen and now numbers over 50 million. In early December 2013, after his three-day visit to China, British Prime Minister David Cameron said that British youngsters should concentrate on learning Chinese to popularize the Chinese language in the UK.

China Book International (CBI)

Books are an important carrier for Chinese culture "going global". Throughout the 30 years before 1978, a total of 9356 books on Chinese culture from 13 categories were translated into 44 languages. Political literatures are a major part, and Chinese contemporary literatures and traditional culture and art are the supplements. Between 1980 and 2009, altogether 9763 Chinese books were translated into foreign languages and publicized. The contents translated saw obvious changes. Books on Chinese culture, history, geography and sceneries amounted to 2426, capturing the first place. Books on politics and laws slid to the 2nd place. Books on art, culture, education, sports, Chinese literature, Chinese economy, languages, Traditional Chinese Medicine, philosophy and religions were also translated for circulation.

China Book International (CBI), started in 2004, aims at supporting domestic and foreign publishing institutions to publish books with themes on China in international market. In 2009, China kicked off the project of translating and publishing cultural literatures to fund the foreign publishing

On May 12th, 2006, the First International Initiative of Chinese Copyright was held in Changsha. "External Promotion Plan of Chinese Books" was a highlight of the initiative.

International influence of Chinese culture

and circulation of academic and literature classics. At the end of 2012, a total of 1095 sponsorship agreements with 486 publishing institutions from 61 countries were signed, covering 2201 books in 38 languages. CBI will also boost China's digital publication to "go global". Over the three years from the implementation of the project of Chinese Publication International Marketing Channel Expansion, a series of outstanding books have entered the distribution network of global 3000 mainstream bookstores. Hundreds of thousand Chinese books are sold in more than 100 Chinese bookstores across the world. Since the establishment of Special Book Award of China in 2005, 34 translators, writers and publishers from a dozen countries have won the honor. In August 2013, the 7th Special Book Award of China was granted to Egyptian translator Mohsen Sayed Fergani, American writer Ezra Feivel Vogel, Argentine writer Jorge Eduardo Malena, Sweden translator Anna Gustafsson Chen, Indonesian publisher Yoza Suryawan and Italian translator Lionello Lanciotti.

Chinese New Year Activities

Spring Festival is the most important festival in China and this holiday contains many Chinese cultural elements, such as valuing kinship and friendship, expressing gratitude and esteem to the nature, commemorating ancestors and stressing traditions, witnesses the evolution of customs and is permeated by joy and love. In January 2010, Ministry of Culture, together with many other departments, held the first overseas Chinese New Year Gala. In 2014, the 5th Chinese New Year Gala, consisting of 506 programs, covered 294 cities of 103 countries and regions. It had a variety of contents, channels and performance forms, such as theater performances, comprehensive performances, parades, cultural temple fairs, overseas Chinese parties, cultural heritage exhibtions, folk art shows, knowledge contests, book fairs, tourism promotions, Spring Festival concerts, Spring Festival Gala on TV, popular music, vogue shows, jewelery and animation design contest, originality and

On January 8th, 2013, Lang Lang's New Year Concert was held in Wuhu, Anhui Province.

creation solicitation, and Spring Festival cultural products development and promotion. Moreover, digital platforms, networks and mobile terminals were applied to introduce Chinese New Year and Spring Festival knowledge, and share the joy of China's traditional festival with the local people. The activities provided important bridges and ties for China's foreign cultural exchanges.

The Chinese People's Association for Friendship with Foreign Countries, Chinese People's Institute of Foreign Affairs, All-China Women's Federation, All-China Youth Federation, various cultural education institutions, cultural art troupes and overseas Chinese have played an active role in non-governmental cultural exchanges. Various summit forums have further deepened the dialogues and communications between thoughts and cultures, and increased mutual understandings and recognitions between China and the world. Some cultural elite interpret Chinese culture with their own images. Characters played by international kungfu star Jackie Chan have become a cultural symbol. In life, he also showcased the wisdom, inclusiveness and kindness of Chinese people and was honored one of global Top 10 Charity Celebrities by Forbes. Chinese young pianist Lang Lang interprets culture with music and is known as "a Chinese name card with impressive characteristics".

Increasing China Media's Ability to Spread to Overseas

In recent years, China's media featuring the *People's Daily*, China Central Television (CCTV) and China Radio International are increasing their overseas influence.

China Today produced by CCTV in 1959 marked the beginning of the efforts to spread Chinese culture through the media. Later programs like *The Silk Road, The Pace of China, Discovering the Yangtze River, The Yellow River, Nourished by the Same River* and *Wild China* showed the world the charm of New China. Since 2009, CCTV has built up a global news network covering the whole world, bringing channels in six different languages to

New building of CCTV on Chaoyang Road in Beijing.

families in more than 170 countries and regions. At present, China Radio International can provide information to the world through new platforms like FM broadcasts, satellite TV, Internet and mobile terminals in 64 languages. China National Radio has produced more programs in languages like Tibetan, Uygur and Kazak and has brought more programs to families of Central Asian countries.

The CIBN was officially launched in May 28, 2012, for business and featured audio-visual interaction, resource-sharing and media convergence. It symbolized the transformation from traditional media to new comprehensive international media in modern times. These media presented real China to the world by introducing Chinese food, tourist attractions and culture in an open way and also responding to international concerns on important areas of China's development such as politics, economy and society. Positive progress and success have been made in building international transmission capacity of China's media.

Compared to strong transmission capacity of western media, China's international communication is still in the beginning stage. Giving equal consideration to both traditional and emerging media, software and hardware construction, China's media has grown at a faster pace with strong communication capacity suiting the country's economic and social development level and international reputation. China's media devoted itself to guarantee its originality and reception to spread China's culture and her voice. It gives a full understanding of modern Chinese society and lets people with different cultural backgrounds touch on China closely and directly.

Joseph Nye, a well-known American scholar, once said that China has recently increased her attraction and influence and soft power through widely spreading her unique culture. Most western counties often praised China's performance in events since 2008 such as the Wenchuan Earthquake, the Beijing Olympic Games and the Global Financial Crisis in particular. In the

Contemporary China's Culture

On June 5th, 2014, as an important event to celebrate the 50th anniversary of diplomatic relations between China and France, "Soul Talk—Sculpture Works Exhibition of Wu Weishan and Claude Abeille " was held at China Culture Center in Paris. It is not only soul talk between the two masters, but also a conversation between culture and art of the two countries.

action in Libya in February 2011, the Chinese government responded positively and rationally and evacuated overseas Chinese to safety. Western media widely acclaimed the Chinese government in this action. The Spanish newspaper *El País* commented that this proved that China is a country that puts people first. L'Agence France-Presse, a French news agency, run a headline that said "China is eager to show concern for workers in Libya".

In March 2004, Chinese president Xi Jinping visited Europe, elaborated the quintessence and unique value system of Chinese culture, China's tribulations in contemporary and modern times and great efforts to pursue for happiness and explained the special value, development, challenges and achievements of Chinese culture. Chinese culture, as a long-standing and well-established culture, has her own development laws and profound historical origins and cannot be abondaned and replaced at will. To realize an all-round,

International influence of Chinese culture

real and complete China needs an objective, historical and multidimensional view. In his speech at UNESCO headquarters, Xi said that culture is colorful and human cultures enjoy communication value due to the diversity. To respond Japanese Prime Minister Shinzo Abe's "value-oriented diplomacy" thought promoted in Europe, Xi Jinping appealed to abondan Cold War thinking and zero-sum game and advocated exchanges, communications and joint progress between different cultures and religions at the 4th Summit of Conference on Interaction and Confidence-Building Measures in Asia.

Communication gives a basis for mutual understanding. Many sinologists had objective attitudes on China because they knew the country well. Ezra Vogel, second director of Harvard's East Asian Research Centre, who was well known as Mr. China, started to study China in the 1960s. He researched and published *Canton Under Communism, One Step Ahead in China: Guangdong Under Reform* and *Deng Xiaoping and the Transformation of China.* He said in the press release of *Deng Xiaoping and the Transformation of China* that this is a book for foreigners like me to "know Deng Xiaoping and that age" and that he hoped that the western world could know more about China.

Professor Rémi Mathieu, a French Sinologist, had a deep affection for Chinese culture and literature. He translated and studied Chinese classics and gave annotations and comments on them. In his book *A Fresh Peony-Image of China in Westerners*, he compares China to a fresh peony whose gorgeous colors and fragrance pervade the world. It symbolized China's spread and the growth of its influence around the world, specially Europe and America. He told western readers in the book that the current China is a perfect result evolved from the combination of Chinese ancient traditions and western modern events.

Two civilizations have experienced a hard course of encounters, clashes conflicts and then fusion, exchanges and learning from each other. He thought that each civilization cannot achieve self-improvement on their own in the process of cultural conflicts and exchanges. The world will be diverse rather than a place of life-or-death struggles. This is the wisdom of China: "harmony in diversity".

The essence of Chinese culture lies in that every form of beauty is unique and that other forms of beauty are openly appreciated. If beauty represents itself with diversity and integrity, the world will be blessed with harmony and unity.

On June 10, 2014, in his first visit to the US, Austrialia Premier Tony Abbott made a keynote speech, calling on the world not to deem China's rise as a threat and stressing that China's economic development to benefit the world.

Recently, the French government's Advanced Audiovisual Council (CSA) officially approved the registration of the "Asia 8" TV station. This cable television network will broadcast around the clock for Chinese-French, overseas Chinese and French people concerned with China. Raymond Sandburg, a China friendly historian and journalist, is the chief editor. This television station will become an important platform for French media to spread positive information of China and added festive atmosphere to the 50th anniversary of diplomatic relations between China and France.

International influence of Chinese culture

Falling Cultural Trade Deficit

After more than 30 years of development, China's cultural trade is gradually diversifying in form and types, dominated by books, audio and video products, overseas performances, films and more. Chinese acrobatics, opera and kungfu have won widespread praise after years of publicity. More and more Chinese cultural master works have gone abroad and found success in international show business. Statistics show that the China Arts & Entertainment Group (CAEG) sent more than 630 performance groups for 33,000 shows to about 80 countries all over the world from 2004 to 2010. These shows were viewed by 70 million people live and 550 million in

On December 13th, 2013, updated version of *Impression of Yunnan* was first performed in Kunming, Yunnan Province. The brand new 4D technology made the background more real.

broadcast. Among these performances, more than 60 percent are commercial shows.

The Chinese film industry is an important part of Chinese culture to "going abroad". Chinese films were confined to the country from 1949 to 1970s. Since the 1980's, an increasing number of Chinese films have gone abroad. Film directors like Zhang Yimou have promoted the transitional development of Chinese films. *Hero* directed by Mr. Zhang in 2002 established the structure of Chinese blockbusters. When it opened in the US in August 2008 it topped the box office for two consecutive weeks earning US$177 million. Since then, Chinese blockbusters have entered into international market. His *House of Flying Daggers* (2004) achieved equal success, earning US$ 93 million in

The Grandmaster, directed by Wong Kar-wai was selected as the opening night film of the 63rd Berlin Film Festival.

International influence of Chinese culture

global office. Led by kung fu films, the overseas box office receipts of Chinese films increased from RMB 500 million in 2002 to RMB 3517 million in 2010. China Film Promotion International was set up in 2004 and played an important role in promoting Chinese films.

North American audiences welcomed *The Grandmaster* (2012), directed by Wong Kar-wai. The *Twelve Chinese Zodiac Signs* set a new record in overseas sales and was shown on screens in 26 countries and regions such as Russia, Korea, Japan, West Asia, the Middle East, Europe and North America. It even topped the box office of Southeast Asia and Russia in the first seven days after its release and had good box office earnings for several years.

In 2008, more than 10,000 hours of Chinese TV programs were sold to over 100 countries and regions, earning a total of about 58.98 million US dollars of exports. By the end of 2010, CCTV International had over 160 million overseas users. When *Beautiful Daughter-in-Law* became a hit in Tanzania, the "China-Africa Film Cooperation Project" led to agreements with 30 African countries. And there will be more than 5000 hours of Chinese TV programs broadcasting in Africa in two years that will be seen by 500 million people.

Thanks to efforts in the past decade, the output structure of copyrighted material from Chinese publications has been optimized and the deficit in China's copyright has been lowered from 15:1 in 2003 to 1.9:1 in 2012. Exports of physical news products maintained continued growth, earning a total of US$ 73.966 million in 2011 and over US$ 100 million in 2012. China has been keeping an obvious trade surplus in printing services. Printing service export industries have earned RMB 68.009 million in processing trade. Three printing industrial zones in Pearl River Delta, Yangtze River Delta and Bohai Rim have become important printing processing bases in the world.

Chinese newspapers such as the magazine *Readers*, *Lady Friend*, the *People's Daily Overseas Edition*, *China Daily* and *Xinmin Evening News* have been internationally recognized. *China Daily* was first published in the US in 1983. It published based on the "the Year of Chinese Enterprises" in 2012 and let the Americans have a deeper understanding of China and Chinese enterprises. The *Readers Overseas Edition* has been sold in over 80 countries and regions all over the world.

China's original online game industry is emerging and is growing fast. In 2010, there were 82 online games researched and developed by 34 Chinese online game enterprises that entered overseas markets, earning US$ 230 million. In 2011, the number of Chinese online game enterprises increased to 66, which developed 92 games and earned US$ 403 million. In 2012, there were more than 131 game enterprises and exports reached US$ 570 million. In the past five years, exports of Chinese online games have increased eight times and some influential brands have appeared.

China encourages cultural enterprises to invest and operate abroad by establishing overseas wholly-owned enterprises, joint ventures,

On October 28th, 2011, the magic cube of "Internet guides Chinese culture going global" exhibited on the 9th China International Digital Content Expo.

International influence of Chinese culture

controlling enterprises and sharing enterprises, and conducting programs like performances, exhibitions and sales activities. China Heaven Creation International Performance Arts Co.,Ltd (CHC) has sent more than 30 groups including acrobatics, dancing, music, magic and Wushu groups to Europe and America. *The Legend of Kungfu*, a large play integrating acrobatics, dancing and Wushu, ran 27 consecutive times in the London Coliseum. The Beijing Wanda Cultural Industry Group acquired AMC of the US at $2.6 billion, becoming the world's largest movie operator with nearly 10% market share in the world. Then Wanda donated $20 million to the Movie Museum of the Academy of Motion Picture Arts and Sciences to be opened in 2017. Jiangsu Phoenix Education Press Limited, a wholly-owned subsidiary of China's Phoenix Publishing & Media Group, acquired the children's books assets and 100% equity of the overseas subsidiaries of American PIL Company at $85 million. It is the first-ever biggest transnational merge in China's publishing industry.

Over the past decade, some 39 presses and publication agencies have either created or acquired 332 publishing business branches overseas.

China is increasing its foreign cultural trade and gradually narrowing its deficit in this area. Statistics show that exports of core cultural products increased from US$ 5.6 billion (2003) to US$ 25.9 billion (2012). However, exports of cultural products are only 1.26% of that of goods, and exports of cultural services are only 2.55% of all service trade. In the international cultural market, China has only a 1.5% market share, while the market share of the US has climbed to an astounding 42.6%. There is still a huge gap between the trade of the US and China. Taking the film business in 2012 as an example, US film production accounted for only 10.1% of the world total, with US$ 10.8 billion domestically, but its overseas box office reached US$ 23.9 billion. The Chinese box office, second only to the US, by contrast, was only US$ 2.7 billion with US$ 1.4 billion sold in the US.

What's worse, there is a big trade deficit in performing arts. The income of one art performance sent overseas is just one-tenth of one introduced from abroad. And the annual income of Chinese business performances overseas is less than US$ 100 million, which is less than that of one famous foreign circus. Animated cartoons from the US and Japan have long dominated China's animation market.

Content is the king of cultural products. Nowadays, Chinese cultural brands with core competence are far from enough and only more products containing Chinese cultural elements and exquisite arts are needed. Can we gain more from cultural trade while spreading the Chinese cultural spirit? In recent times, Chinese stories are attracting attention. Animated cartoons Mulan and Kung Fu Panda caught global eyeballs. Modern China, capable to offer products for 124 countries, has enough reasons to tell her own stories well and present renowned cultural brands to the world.

On March 17, 2014, China released Opinions on Accelerating Foreign Cultural Trade to offer financial supports like credit, bonds, insurance, guarantee and foreign exchange administration, not only supporting and developing state-owned cultural enterprises going global but also encouraging the development of non-public export-oriented cultural enterprises so that various enterprises could survive and develop independently in overseas cultural markets through their own features and advantages and at the same time reduce their dependence on the Chinese government in terms of cultural exchanges. Encouraged by the great cultural industrial incentives, Chinese cultural industrial personages confidently applauded, "another spring for cultural industry is coming." How to grasp the "golden springtime" and convert profound Chinese culture into modern high-quality cultural products? We should learn from the operation patterns of mature western markets by strengthening markets and marketing consciousnesses, expanding platforms and channels for cultural exports, as well as the market share of Chinese cultural products and services. Cultural competition focuses on lofty spirit, exquisite originality, human-friendly design, emotional story, and people-centered user experience. Only through a deep understanding to culture, market and demand can we produce products with high added cultural value and improve enterprises' cultural competitiveness.

Cultural innovation power is a globally recognized "cultural hard currency". China needs greater efforts to enable her cultural products to occupy global market like her industrial products.

Conclusion

Conclusion

Culture is the blood and soul of a nation and also a solid foundation for a nation to step into the future with confidence. The Action Plan to *Promote Cultural Development by Policies formulated* by the United Nations Educational Scientific and Cultural Organization (UNESCO) points out that a nation's development should be defined in terms of culture and cultural prosperity is the ultimate goal of development of a nation.

The Communist Party of China analyzed the role of culture in the development of society and indicated that a country or a nation will stand towering in the world community only when it has its own unique culture and the rich inner world of its people, gives full play to national spirits. Since the foundation of New China in 1949, especially recent decades, China endeavors to promote the development and prosperity of its culture in areas of cultural programs, cultural industries, its contents and forms, as well as its system and management. A breakthrough and great-leap-forward development is achieved in education and technology and religious harmony is realized. Through these achievements, China could stand among the great cultural nations, as well as political and economic powers and its cultural influence overseas is growing.

However, China's cultural development as a whole is lower in quality and unequal, with irrational structure of cultural industries. Instructional barriers which restrict the development of culture and science still exist. And there is great room to improve cultural products to meet people's various and multi-levels of demands. We need to build a modern cultural market system so as to further liberate and develop cultural productive forces, improve the supply capacity of cultural products and services and standardize and equalize basic public cultural services. We should also promote the integration of science and culture and speed up establishing cultural innovation systems in the new reality of rapid

Contemporary China's Culture

development of modern information technology and communication. The Sixth Plenary Session of the 17th Central Committee of the Party made cultural power construction a national strategy. It reflected the importance and urgency of building modern Chinese culture.

Today's China needs to improve its soft cultural power, which refers to the cohesion, charisma and influence of a country or a nation built through its core values, and cultural production, trade and services. China is a large country with a long history of culture, so it is one of the world's toughest problems to transform China from an agricultural society to an industrialized and urbanized society.

What's surprising, is that China finished the job of economic development in 30 years, something western countries took hundreds of years to do. During this time, many social problems appeared. So our government, the society and the people joined together in an effort to solve these problems. We should strengthen the ideological consensus and cultural identity, which can improve national cohesiveness and the country's cultural centripetal force. We need cultural consciousness so as to improve the thickness, depth and height of Chinese civilization. We need education, science and technology, cultural industries and innovation to support the course of Chinese economic structure transformation. The central part of Chinese cultural reform and development is to inspire cultural creativity of the nation for a civilized and advanced society should be a society where material and spiritual civilization achieve mutual improvement. And a modern powerful country should be a nation where its economy, politics, culture, society and ecological civilization develop collaboratively. Thus, it is urgent to play a leading role in culture, educate the people, serve society and promote the development of society.

Overseas, China's resurgence on the international stage as an important power is one of the most notable events today. China, as the world's second largest economy, has become a new engine which drives world economic

Conclusion

development and has made remarkable progress militarily. But what comes after the rise of an emerging country is China making increasing contributions to the international community, but it is not treated with the respect it deserves. There are sometimes biased voices opposing China. So Chinese culture should go abroad and let foreigners know the real China and the essence of Chinese culture.

Lee Kuan Yew, Singapore's former Prime Minister and Senior Minister, published on August 6, 2013, *A Man's View of the World*, in which he draws on his experience over the past decades and insight to offer his views on today's world and what it might look like in 20 years. In this book, he describes a China that remains obsessed with control from the center on its way to an unstoppable rise. He said that for 5000 years, the Chinese have always believed that the country is safe only when the center is strong. A weak center means confusion and chaos. Every Chinese person knows that and it is the fundamental principle of Chinese people. Some westerners hope that China will become a democratic country in the western tradition. But that is impossible, because China, a nation of 1.3 billion people, has its own development pattern which is different from that of western countries. Cultural diversity is a basic feature of today's world and an important driving force for the progress of human civilization. As Chinese culture goes abroad, more people in the world will understand the spirit of China, which loves peace and treating neighbors kindly so as to ease international fears about its rise.

Inheriting an excellent culture while absorbing excellent cultural achievements, forging a cultural core with humanistic charm and cultural heritages to match the position of a great country and developing and innovating Chinese culture in accordance to the requirements of the development of modern society and of our people are parts of cultural modernization and a mission of contemporary Chinese cultural construction. At present, cultural construction has become a national cause and it aims to make

Chinese society more active, more orderly and moe harmonious in continuous innovation and aims to make sure that the Chinese people will be happier. It also aims to seek common points while reserving differences and make a concerted effort and mutual cooperation with other countries to jointly promote the development and prosperity of world culture and discovering that every form of beauty has its uniqueness while appreciating other forms of beauty with openness.